Ladies
of the
Avenue

Ladies of the Avenue

by

Patricia E. Tierney

**BARTHOLOMEW
HOUSE
LTD**

BARTHOLOMEW HOUSE LTD.
First Printing . . . . October 1971

Library of Congress Catalog Card Number: 73-155026
International Standard Book Number: 87794-027-4

CONTENTS

The End   11

I   *"Why IS a Nice Girl Like Me . . ."*   13

II   *Will the Real Copywriter Please Stand Up?*   17

III   *Exposure as a Way of Life*   26

IV   *The Lady Account Man*   34

V   *It Worked for Eve*   42

VI   *Between a Nun and a Whore*   53

VII   *"Fly with the Ones Who Gunned Your Sons"*   62

VIII   *One Man's Ink Blot*   74

IX   *Can't We Make It Habit-Forming?*   81

X   *"To Begin with, She's . . ."*   94

XI   *Across the Hudson and Into the Woods*   104

XII   *People in Palm Beach Have Bad Breath, Too*   113

XIII   *If a Man Asks, Hang up*   123

XIV   *I Never Called It a Cure*   134

XV   *They're Not All Difficult . . . Some Are Impossible*   146

XVI   *Ready Whenever You Are, C.B.*   156

XVII   *Around the World in Ninety Seconds*   168

XVIII   *Cinéma Vérité in Cincinnati*   179

XIX   *Out of the Sandbox, Into the Board Room*   186

XX   *Shortsighted Memos and Blind Carbons*   197

XXI   *As Long as You Spell My Name Right*   206

XXII   *The Migratory Birds*   212

XXIII   *You Don't Have To Be Black To Enjoy Prejudice*   227

XXIV   *How I Got Resigned*   235

XXV   *Some of My Best Friends Still Are*   245

Ladies of the Avenue

To the first lady in my life

Evelyn MacDonald Tierney

The End

"I was shocked to hear you've resigned," the art director said to me.

"Don't give it a second thought," I assured him. "I'm a little upset, but I haven't resigned."

But by the time the third person had called me that afternoon to say how dismayed he was that I'd resigned, I decided to trace the rumor back to its source. It was Harry, the hatchet man for the new order that claimed they were making a clean sweep of the creative department. (Never put a broom or a hatchet into the hands of the untrained—he was also sweeping out half of the agency's accounts. But no matter.)

"Listen Harry, stop telling people I resigned," I used as an opener.

"But I've accepted your resignation," the hatchet reposted.

"You can't accept a resignation I never offered! Now you get back on the phone and call all those people and admit that you fired me."

CHAPTER I

"Why IS a Nice Girl Like Me . . ."

At first glance it could have been the opening orgy scene that has now become *de rigueur* for modern novels: a darkened bedroom high in one of the posh towers that dominates the East Side landscape, the lights of the city twinkling below, and, of course, a king-sized bed. On the bed, the three of us: Bob, Dennis, and me. A voyeur would have been disappointed as his eyes became adjusted to the dim light; he'd have seen that we were all completely dressed, including Dennis who was wearing his best collar—imported from Italy via the Saks pet shop. Even more disappointing to the voyeur, we were all participating in America's second most popular indoor sport: TV-watching.

Propped up on the bed, surrounded by loved ones, there I was, watching myself lock wits with David Susskind on the flickering screen. (The show had been taped several days earlier.) It was one of those ubiquitous talk shows where a bunch of people with similar problems or axes to grind rap with the moderator. It was the last show of the season and the writers had evidently hit bottom: Our common shtick that night was being unemployed. I qualified for the panel, having been bested by an agency creative director—an insecure type who couldn't think of any other way to get the client to prefer his efforts to mine. After all, you can hardly fire *clients* for a thing like that.

"The Plight of the Unemployed Executive" was the theme of the show, but my friends kept referring to it as "The Failure Forum"! Though I was eminently suited to such a show, I had agreed to appear on it not so I could beat my breast in living rooms across the country, but rather to beat the drum for my first novel. When the doors of agency creative departments had slammed shut on anyone who wasn't under thirty or on drugs, I had taken to my bed with Smith, Corona, and Marchant, and the four of us had turned out *Naked Encounter*. It was a fictionalized version of all those soul-searching, touch-me-feel-me things, written not out of any strong feelings about them but just to see if I had the self-discipline to write sixty or seventy thousand consecutive words. Up until that time, the longest commercially successful writing I had done was a ninety-second TV spot. As it turns out, desperation works wonders with one's self-discipline, and in no time I had completed my first novel.

Knowing that TV appearances by authors always hypo their book sales, I jumped at the chance to appear on *Open End*. At the screening interview, I made much of the difficulties of enforced poverty—which is a tough story to tell when a glance at your card shows you are tucked away in a pad on Sutton Place. But I emphasized the down side of the picture and after a couple of coaching sessions—I was not to mention I owned my apartment nor that my stock portfolio had weathered Wall Street's latest storms 25 per cent better than the Dow Jones—they gave me the nod.

It was my first attempt at plugging a book and it hardly qualified as a complete success. How many sales my appearance generated hasn't been reckoned yet, but mentioning that

I'd written *Naked Encounter* did result in three calls from people who wanted me to write their life stories, several calls from deviates, and a fan letter from an Italian poet. It wasn't a total loss. But as I watched myself trying to field the questions being shot at me by the Sunday night quarterback at my side, I wondered. Why hadn't I talked about my book sooner in the show? Why hadn't I mentioned the publication date or at least the name of the publisher? Why hadn't I told that harassing hirsute hippy who had it in for advertising practitioners that the taxes I paid last year had provided the government with enough funds to support three full-time civic do-gooders at his level? I thought back to the previous week when we'd taped the show to find some excuse for my failings.

It had been one of those incredibly hot and humid days that New York City does so well, and since the local studio was under siege by strikers, we were on our way out to Philadelphia to tape the show. There we were, in the back of an air-conditioned limousine, three people whose combined salaries had been about $120,000. Now, thanks to a government-sponsored depression, we were all on the beach. (You remember the rule: It's a recession when you know someone out of work; it's a depression when *you're* out of work.)

We were hurtling down the Jersey Turnpike in an unseemly show of haste when the show's producer dropped the first bomb of the day: Someone had silver-tongued the Screen Actors Guild into swallowing some kind of story about the Susskind show being educational TV. That meant none of us was to receive a single sou for all our on-camera hand-wringing. Not even a dinner allowance! A long pause followed that announcement and a lot of looking out the window. One of the highlights of the Jersey landscape that afternoon was David Susskind's block-long Mercedes panting at the roadside for want of a spare tire. David had taken off by thumb for Phila-

15

delphia, his chauffeur told us. Just retribution, I thought, for his exploitation of us downtrodden unemployed. After all, *he* was being paid to appear on the show and from the length of that Mercedes, evidently rather generously.

Things didn't improve when I walked into the studio that evening and discovered from the seating arrangement that I was going to be photographed from my bad side. (Hard core unemployed or not, you can still worry about some pretty inconsequential things if you try.) I asked one of the staff if I could sit in the opposite chair. He glanced down at the little chart on the table in front of Susskind's chair and said kindly, "Sure, if you don't mind being called Bob Margulies all evening."

Nor was my best brought out when David's first words to me were, "Why doesn't a nice girl like you get married and forget this business?" With the number of writers he has on tap, to open with a chestnut like that convinced me he must have suffered sunstroke on the Turnpike before the Citgo truck picked him up. I settled back in my plastic chair and tried to prepare myself for the coming battle of wits, but as far as I was concerned, the most provocative question of the evening had been asked before the cameras started to roll: "Why doesn't a nice girl like me. . . ."

CHAPTER II

Will the Real Copywriter Please Stand Up?

Like so many other young ladies of gentle upbringing, I had been graduated from a fine old New England university totally unprepared to do anything for which there was a legal market. I was also just as totally undecided about what I really wanted to be when I grew up. (I still am, but that's neither here nor there.) Ever since exposure in my formative years to a Marlene Dietrich movie whose title is lost in the never-never land of the past, I had deep down inside wanted to be a torch singer; but it would have been hard to distinguish my shape in a sequin gown from the post I intended to lean against, and I was not only tone deaf, but unable to carry a tune. So though it has always seemed like a delicious idea, it did seem like an ill-advised direction for me to take.

My mother, who felt that no matter what else a girl decided to do with her life, she should be able to support herself, thought teaching was the ideal career for me. She felt it was one of the few depression-proof careers since it was unlikely that children would ever be born knowing how to read and write. But somehow the Rosalind Russell movies always appealed to me a lot more than the Martha Scott ones, and Roz never played a school teacher.

17

The idea of being a writer had crossed my mind a few times in the course of my adolescence. When I confided this secret dream to the dean assigned to counsel me, she advised me quite wholeheartedly not to consider English, the obvious choice, as a major. "From what I read in your column, you obviously know the mechanics of writing. What you really need is material to write about." From this remark I assumed she was not overly pleased with the gossipy chatter column I was lining out every Friday for the school paper. She advised me to study history, psychology, or sociology.

History was too full of dates for someone with the sievelike mind I'd been blessed with, and at that particular university psychology was more animal than social and required a lot of frog contact which had little or no appeal. So by a process of elimination, and the fact it was the easiest major on campus, I opted for sociology with a psychology minor. It was, oddly enough, just the right combination of courses to make advertising my cup of tea.

Maybe in the big Midwestern universities, the city diploma factories, or the upstate football academies, they were giving courses designed to prepare you for advertising, but not in the ivy- and tradition-laden campus where I matriculated. They had far loftier, or at least vaguer, ideals. "To prepare you to take your rightful place in a thinking society" was their aim. The aim of my fellow undergraduates seemed to be to prepare themselves to hold their own in a drinking society. Actually neither aim was far off the mark, and neither was a total loss for someone destined for Madison Avenue.

My very first job in an advertising agency (and this one never landed on any résumé) was in the traffic department of a small shop. I had gotten the job, which consisted of typing out forms, by inadvertently lying rather magnificently about my typing skills. (To this day it remains an undeveloped skill,

18

and I must search out each key with my eye first and then my finger.) Knowing absolutely nothing about typing or shorthand when I filled out the form at the employment agency, I listed my typing speed at one hundred words a minute and my shorthand at one hundred and fifty. Needless to say, I had no trouble landing this plum of a job which I believe paid something on the order of $32.00 a week. At the end of three weeks, it became obvious to them that I couldn't type, and obvious to me that the head of the department was not only a lush but a deviate. So ended my first job in advertising.

I explained to the employment agency that I felt I was wasting my talents in such menial work and was really after a career—not a job. My next position carried the highest title and the lowest salary I was ever to work for again: I was the assistant to the advertising director of a large lingerie manufacturer and was making the magnificent salary of $35.00 a week.

I might have been taking my place in a thinking society, but at that salary I was hardly in a position to enjoy it very much. The advertising director I worked for was a tiny older woman who had the patience of a saint with me and taught me one of the first cardinal rules of the ad game. It is the duty of the agency's account executive to wine, dine, and entertain the client. As I sat nibbling on my peanut butter sandwich, I would watch this tiny tyro take off for one posh restaurant after another, accompanied by the agency's account executive. It was barely two years before I'd had my fill of peanut butter sandwiches and lingerie salesmen.

My next job doubled my salary and landed me in the hallowed halls of Batten, Barton, Durstine & Osborn where I started out in publicity, and then was switched to TV when there was a sudden need for warm bodies in that department.

It was the best of all times and the best of all places to learn TV and advertising. For it was that moment in time when TV was just being discovered as an advertising medium. Clients who had for decades been splitting their budgets between magazines, newspapers, and radio threw themselves into TV with abandon. And since it was such a new toy, there was no such thing as an experienced practitioner in the field. Oddly enough, the greybeards in the creative department who had risen to fame and fortune on their print advertising campaigns were the most reluctant to try their hands at writing for TV. They resented the move of their clients' money from print to TV and instead of following it, they seemed to feel if they buried their heads in the sand long enough, the whole blinking little black box would go up in a puff of smoke. It was an amazingly bad decision from their point of view, and even more amazing was their persistence in that point of view for so long. And yet the agency kept them on in their exalted positions and at their inflated salaries, while the advertising for the agency's biggest accounts was being conceived and executed by a bunch of young kids—not one of whom was making $12,000 a year.

In fact, at a salary of around $100 a week, I was writing all the television for five major accounts with a cumulative billing of close to $30 million a year. I never again worked for so little nor have I ever again had the creative responsibility for so much annual billing. By the time I left BBDO I had worked on close to thirty accounts. It was a great way to learn the business, and since everyone else was learning right along with you, nobody thought it was odd that all that billing should have been placed in such untried though willing hands.

I left BBDO after five really great years, lured to Benton & Bowles by the $10,000 a year salary that seemed like such a prize in those long ago days. After a few years there, I was brought to D'Arcy by better than twice that amount, and the money just kept getting better and better. Nobody had any nicer things to say about advertising than I did in those golden years. Whether or not I had prepared for it properly didn't seem to matter. I adored advertising, and nothing in all those years could have led me to believe that it was anything less than a mutual affair.

Not every lady of the Avenue got into the business because she had prepared for nothing else, but it certainly wasn't a bad start. Lots of the ladies in the corner offices today started in the secretarial pool. I know one writer who got into copy because of her camp counselor. He had heard her mooning about advertising when she was running around the woods in her rompers, and a few years later, when she had graduated from college, he suggested she go to Ogilvy & Mather where a fellow camper was entrenched. They rapped for a while, and I guess rubbed a few sticks together. The chemistry was right, she took the copy aptitude test and came out a winner. I suppose camp is as good a place as any to prepare for advertising.

A friend of mine prepped for a career in advertising at one of the more select academies for young women in the South. She tells me she was forced into advertising by a stubborn streak of New England thrift that had not been quieted by all those years among the magnolia blossoms. After spending half her life married to an ad man, she hated to waste all that experience. "Thank God he wasn't a brain surgeon or a nuclear physicist," she has often said.

One copy chief I know started out as a secretary at J. Walter Thompson back in the days when they were sexually divided: The ladies in the flowered hats held the creative reins on half the accounts, and the men in grey flannel handled the others. As my friend admits now, it was the perfect place for a girl fresh from the convent school. It was in more ways than one. Along with sixty other young hopefuls, she had taken the Thompson copy aptitude test and was one of ten selected to

21

take their copy training course. It was a course famous in the industry but it, like the ladies in the flowered hats themselves, never made it through the swinging sixties. The "course" consisted of spending your lunch hours worshipfully at the feet of one of the behatted ladies while she passed on what she knew about advertising like some holy oracle, and spending your evenings doing assignments—anything from sample ads to whole campaigns. My friend and one other girl survived this trial by fire. They were rewarded at the end of the year-long course with the lofty title of junior copywriter and a desk in the center of the floor, surrounded by dozens of others of equally low estate, at the beck and call of any copy writer who needed fresh blood or fresh thinking on an account. They were moved from account to account with head-spinning regularity. Their copy was used and taken credit for by almost anyone who happened along in a flowered hat. And through it all they were neither to question nor object. I told you the convent school was a great training ground for JWT in those halcyon days. But despite all the campaign filching and the other initiation rites, she survived three years there, put together a proof book that was all hers and mind boggling in its diversity, and on the strength of it was hired by Young & Rubicam—not known for their big spending ways—at twice her Thompson salary. And the beautiful part of it is that she doesn't regret one of those ghastly mind-bending days at JWT.

Another friend of mine who cut her copy teeth at Y&R has almost as hair-raising a tale of breaking in. Evidently if you didn't break down under the initiation rites, you'd broken in. She had been a secretary for a creative director, doing all the typing for the print and TV output of eight writers, including pasting up the storyboards, and dreaming of being a copywriter. So out of the munificence of their hearts, they let her write some live TV commercials for the Captain Kangaroo show. Sure they let her write the commercials, and they let her take them to the client and sell them, and then on her lunch hour they let her take them to the network for continuity clearance. Of course they didn't let her off any of her secretarial work at the time, but they did let her write copy, and that was a heady enough experience to carry her through it all.

They don't make copywriters like that anymore. Far be it from me to say they don't make them as good, it's just that they don't make them *that* way. The new breed seems to drift in, dressed for a masquerade, using for credentials the kind of things you see scrawled on the walls of latrines.

When TV first became a threat to the print writers, the big agencies set up separate TV departments to handle the copy and art for this maverick medium. Years later when it became obvious, despite the protestations of the print mavens, that TV was not going to disappear, the agencies gradually dissolved their separate TV departments and merged them with their print departments. I remember one day at B & B when the two copy departments became one. The top creative guy called us all together and announced, "From now on, no one in this room is a TV writer or a print writer. You're all advertising writers." It was as painless as that. At least in theory it was. What actually happened was that you ended up with a lot of copy supervisors who had never even read a TV commercial passing judgment on them. (Would you believe one of these actually trying to *sing* the video directions?)

For a friend of mine who had worked only on television, the transition was not all that easy. She was given her first print assignment, went into her office, and burst into tears. Her copy supervisor found her in this state of disarray. When she told him she didn't think she was capable of writing a print ad, he told her, "Don't be silly. Just think of the ad as a freeze frame." She now works strictly in print, and to this day she thinks of every ad as a freeze frame or key scene in a TV commercial.

A lot of the ladies of the Avenue made it into copy and often into the corner offices by working their way up inside the agency in which they may have started as a secretary, typist, or general lackey. But an even greater number, the ones who had no patience for the long haul, used one agency as a stepping stone into another. A friend of mine, who worked for years in one agency as a secretary and later as a writer, says the biggest mistake you can make is to stay on as a writer where you once were a secretary. Even if *you* ever forget you started out there as a lackey, somebody's sure to remember, and you never do get paid what you're really worth. A lot of people must agree with her theory because the number who grab off that copy writer's title and then hit the Avenue almost immediately with their proof books is enormous. In fact, a great many of them take to the streets with a proof book long before they've ever written an ad of their own. Grey Advertising, for instance, was notorious for having one really marvelous collection of proofs in a book that was being peddled all over town by their mail boys who were trying to pass as copywriters. And the résumés they used had to be their finest hour —creatively speaking.

This is often the case even with experienced writers. In fact, the more experience you have selling potions, soaps, and appliances, obviously, the better able you are to sell yourself. That's what a résumé is—an ad for yourself. Because the government regulatory agents have no control over this form of self-assessment, the lyric extremes to which some writers go in their résumés is unmatched by any other form of expression.

Most writers put together a basic résumé listing the accounts they've worked on (and in some cases under this heading go a lot of showpiece accounts on which they had never worked), and their little triumphs and awards. But other writers prefer to use a different résumé for every job they go after, slanting their experience and qualifications for the job that's being offered. In theory that's a great idea, but if you're ever called for a job on an unnamed account, you're left wondering what kind of a résumé to pull out of your book.

I once interviewed a writer who found herself in this embarrassing position. Trying to guess by the ads on my wall the account I was hiring for, she leafed madly through a file of variously slanted résumés tucked in among her proofs. It was an interview vaguely reminiscent of that TV game show *To Tell the Truth*. I sat there wondering, as she flipped through her résumés, if the real writer would ever stand out from that crowd in her proof book.

CHAPTER III

Exposure as a Way of Life

Having spent all but the first few weeks of your life exposed to advertising in all shapes and forms, you usually feel pretty confident about your first attempt at it. You do, that is, until you have it typed. No critic, no creative director, no client, can be as devastating as that first exposure of your work to your typist.

In order to understand just how demoralizing an experience it is, you must first understand with whom you are dealing. In all my years of experience in agencies, the girls who typed my ads—whether they were part of a great anonymous typing pool or my very own special secretary—invariably fell into one of two categories: Either they were frightfully ambitious and after my job, or they were typing merely to keep their hands busy while they planned their upcoming wedding to some youth in Queens.

Having had an overabundance of the latter, I have vicariously lived through more weddings, right down to agonizing over the most minute detail of the table settings at the reception, then have the bridal counselors at Bendel's and Bergdorf's combined. Don't let the current discussions about the waning popularity of marriage and elaborate weddings mislead you. There are still armies of these young women who dream of and plan for the big day from the time they are big enough to lift the latest catalogue-sized issue of *Bride's Magazine* off the shelf.

Despite what you may read in your favorite chatter column about the Beautiful People, marriage among the girls who type ad copy is not something to be rushed into lightly or quickly. How much time and thought actually go into the choosing of the man involved I've no idea, since that always seems to have been taken care of before they hit the job market. But the care and agonizing that goes into every tiny detail of the wedding, honeymoon, trousseau, and first apartment—that I can vouch for.

With so many more important things on her mind, you have to consider yourself lucky if she is able to snatch enough time from her planning to transcribe your pathetic offerings onto "Final" forms. The biggest mistake you as a writer can make, and the most harm you can do yourself, is to expect some kind of reaction to your efforts from these girls. They type with all the understanding, if not the accuracy, of a robot. And no matter how much your little vignette cracked up your peers along copy row, don't expect it to get even a slight smile from your typist. She is there to plan her forthcoming nuptials and to type, in that order—not to react to your ads. A friend of mine, so frustrated by months of trying to elicit a reaction from her typist, included her day's grocery list in among the copy just to get a rise. It not only didn't get a rise out of the girl, it appeared in its entirety (with cauliflower incorrectly spelled).

But if you think the lack of reaction is hard to take, you haven't sampled the overreaction on the part of the other genre of typist. She is fresh from school or some minor triumphs on the pages of her hometown newspaper, and she has taken the job in the steno pool or as your secretary just to get into an agency. She is fully confident that the moment she turns in her first piece of copy, she will be whisked away from her typewriter and ensconced in a corner office by an impressed and grateful copy chief who will credit her with "saving the big account." Don't for one minute think that the dreams born in all those Ginger Rogers movies have died in the hearts of the young. They may not even know who Ginger Rogers was, but they buy that rags-to-riches dream just as big as our simpler generation before them did.

These lovelies, who are determined either to take your job or the one above yours, work their magic in many different ways. All of them are equally devastating to a writer's fragile hold on sanity. The kinder ones come directly to you with what they consider improvements to your copy, your visuals, or your concepts. "Don't you think it would be a better commercial if the housewife said . . ." is a usual opener. At first you may react in a flustered way, admitting you hadn't thought of that and agreeing maybe she's right, but after a few such encounters, you are ready for her and with a little luck and a lot of bravado can be one up on her. By now, in anticipation of her contributions, you have thought of every possible remark the beleaguered housewife could make under the circumstances. This effort has cut a good bit into your sleeping time, but you've got to maintain the upper hand in these exchanges or concede the ground. Then when she comes in with her suggestion, you are ready to snap back, "Of course, I thought of that, too, but it doesn't work as well because. . . ." If there is no reason under the sun why her line doesn't work as well as yours, merely say firmly, "But I think my line works much better there." After all, you are the writer, and she, at least for the next few minutes, is still the typist. I became so adept at delivering this *coup de grâce* to unsolicited copy contributions that I once lost a perfectly marvelous secretary, a really lovely girl, and bright, too. But she finally tired of our game, threw up her hands, and went back to the Midwest where she married an heir to the Purina Ralston fortune. I imagine she's happy as a clam, mentally making suggestions every time she picks up an ad or watches a commercial.

So much for the girls whose surface ambition is merely the improvement of your commercial or "our commercial," as they soon begin to think of it. The really devious ones give you back your neatly typed manuscripts without a word, keeping an extra carbon for themselves. This is then attached to their own effort and presented to your immediate superior or the head of all creation, if she has cast loving eyes in that direction. Now put yourself in the copy chief's shoes. Presented with two similar pieces of copy (these girls are usually not strong on innovation), one written by a $20,000 or $30,000 per annum writer and the other by a $150 a week typist, wouldn't *you* be tempted to give the little lady a crack at the job? And that's how a lot of girls make it out of the typing pool and into the office next to yours. *Next* to yours if you're lucky, yours if you're not.

Sometimes these girls who type your scripts actually convince themselves (or at least someone else) that they have had a far greater hand in the final ad or commercial than the transcribing of it from yellow to white paper. I had a secretary once who took a portfolio of the ads she had typed for me to another agency and got a damned good salary as a writer, considering she'd not written a word herself. When I mentioned this and the price she got to my group head, he said, "Be grateful she got such good money on the strength of your ads. Wouldn't you feel a lot worse if she'd been turned down with them?" There's always room in the ad world for Pollyannas like that. This practice of passing off the work of others as your own is so widespread it hardly bears mentioning here, but it seems to have been carried to its extreme recently in an interview a friend of mine was having with a job applicant. Leafing through the girl's proof book, she happened on an ad she herself had written some time before.

"Funny you should have this ad in your book. I didn't think this product was ever at your old agency."

"Oh, part of the account has been there for years."

"But this particular product never was."

"Are you sure?"

"Quite. And that's why I'm wondering why this ad is in your proof book. You know and I know you didn't write it. As a matter of fact, I did."

"Well, it's in the book because I did work on part of that account, and I *could* have written it." You see now why the truth-in-advertising legislation is having such sticky going?

Though the uses and misuses of proof books along the Avenue are legendary, it is not always the *owner* of the book who is the culprit. Portfolio pilfering is especially rampant by those agencies with cosmetic accounts where the pressure is ever on them to come up with fresh copy claims for new products.

"Leave your book" is the opening line, and whether it comes from the flesh peddler, the receptionist, or the agency's head of all creation, the results are the same: When you pick up your book, it is dog-eared and thumb-marked beyond recognition. In the desperate search for new material, the plastic sleeves of your book have been frantically pawed and fleeced for hidden jingles, a fresh statistic, etc. This can be a big problem for young writers; without much published advertising to their credit, most of their proof books are spec ads. But even experienced writers include in their books favorite ads which never saw the light of print. There's no protection from it, and it's an exposure you can't avoid if you're "looking."

A friend of mine, now a copy chief but at the time just a

writer for J. Walter Thompson, was sent to see the Creative Goddess at a really big cosmetic house. The CG never lifted her eyes from the proof book as she leafed through it. Closing the book, the CG said she'd found nothing that looked promising and the interview ended right there. Needless to say, my friend was more than a bit disappointed. Toward the back of her proof book she'd put in some exploratory work she'd done on color campaigns for Cutex. Included was a campaign for those "Palomino Pales," complete with references to "Runaway Reds" and the slogan "Beat a stampede to your store."

Sure it sounds familiar. Everybody saw the campaign with the nude lovely in the field with the palomino. A few months after the interview, national advertising broke for "Palomino Pales" and "Runaway Reds," but it wasn't run by Cutex. I know it could have been a coincidence, but when an idea doesn't look promising in a proof book, it's funny how great it seems when you think of it later yourself.

At one agency, I had a girl typing my scripts who was driven by some mad urge to be the first one out of the typing pool and into a writer's cubicle. Although she is now a good friend of mine, at that time she was a real cross to bear. There seemed to be no end to the number of ways she could suggest to improve my efforts. And she was not a girl to take no lying down, sitting up, or standing. At that time—even as today—it was a lot easier to get writers than it was to get typists, so it behooved you to keep a civil tongue in your cheek when dealing with these masters of the keyboard. However, you could talk any way you pleased to a writer. Writers took direction or to the street. So in order to relieve the constant pressure of this girl upon all of us, we promoted her from typist to junior writer where she had to, if not sit in awe of us, at least listen. She has long since left Madison Avenue for marriage and motherhood, and she has at present a fairly remunerative side-line inventing and selling games. She'd always been great at playing them.

That all girls don't make it into copy through the typing pool was mentioned earlier. But my favorite story of the making of a writer is the one about the young art school graduate who applied for and obtained a job in the art department paste-up room at N. W. Ayer in Philadelphia. She was so accident prone—between tipping over paste pots, and slicing off parts of layouts and her fingers—that she was quickly shifted to a typewriter as a copy cub. You see, to have fired her so soon after hiring her would have reflected badly on the judgment of those who did it. How well she would have done had she stayed in art we will never know, but she's doing fantastically well as an associate creative director now.

If you can survive the trial by indifference and aggression waged by the girls who type your copy, almost any subsequent criticism seems inconsequential. It's a rare ad indeed that doesn't run into a little flak somewhere along the way, from creative directors, account executives, or clients. And then when everyone's demands have been met, and this creation by committee finally does hit the magazine page or the tiny home screen, come even more reactions: from the consumers who do or do not react as planned, from your friends and peers who know that it's your account, and from the trade press.

For those copywriters in the business for the glory as well as the gain, the ultimate exposure has recently been the rapidly proliferating festivals where endless awards are given out. What is truly remarkable about these coveted awards is the fact that so many of them are given to advertising that is either not successful for the client or is being run by a client so unhappy that he is about to pick up his account and move to another shop. The number of industry competitions, festivals, and awards has increased with such rapidity in the past few years that several large agencies have announced that they would compete no more. It was unfortunate that Ogilvy should announce the setting up of an award for the most effective advertising so late in the game. It was an award that was long overdue.

If the awards committees are the ultimate exposure a writer or art director gets, the ultimate exposure the agency itself endures is the newly popular game of going public. P.K.L. was the first to do it, and they started a stampede that was finally slowed only by the 1970 sinking spell of the stock market. By opening up their books, if nothing else, to public scrutiny, they were able to do in public what they could never have done in private: turn a really quick buck for the insiders, and spread the risk among a larger number of outsiders.

Never having worked at an agency that went public, I was interested to find out how such a transition affected the agency's personnel. So I called up a girl I knew only slightly (how well can you get to know someone you only meet swinging on the next trapeze at exercise class?) who had been with the big hot shop that went public. She remembered stretching muscles with me, and we chatted about a couple of mutual friends. But when I told her I wanted to find out what it was like to be at an agency when it went public, she said she'd rather not talk about it. It was all over, she'd like to forget it, and anyhow she was still in the business (although no longer at that agency). Now this is a girl who has to be one of the very best writers in the business. The story she wants to forget is actually pretty much in the public domain, but if she wants it buried, far be it from me to disinter it. Fear is as much a part of the air as the pollution along Madison Avenue.

CHAPTER IV

The Lady Account Man

For every little girl who crawls out of her sandbox determined to be an account executive, at least a hundred opt for being another Albert Schweitzer or an astronaut. It's just as well, because rarest of all birds along Madison Avenue is the Lady Account Man. The name itself is a paradox.

The most common way for girls to break out of the steno pool and into copywriting is by taking on the added duties of a young writer while still carrying on their full-time work as a secretary or typist. But that just doesn't work for fledgling account executives. You can't take on the added duties of an account exec and squeeze them into your lunch hour or your evening hours. Well, actually, you could, but you'd have to have an account pretty much in your hip pocket to pull that off. And if you did have one tied up like that, it's most unlikely you'd be working your fingertips to the bone at any lackey work. With the way out of the steno pool blocked, most lady account men come into the agency end of the business from the client side. After a client has shown enough faith in a lovely to place the responsibility for all his advertising in her hands for several years, then *maybe* an agency will let her in on the fringes of some account. But only maybe.

The idea that women should do two jobs for the price of one is one that dies hard at the agencies. One of the lady account executives I once had the pleasure of working with not only had full account responsibilities, but PR responsibilities as well. As you may have guessed, she had worked her way up onto the account executive floor from the PR department. She was in so solid with the client that when the account supervisor was looking for a new account executive, he asked her for recommendations. Knowing just how well she could handle the job, she suggested herself. (Shy flowers just don't make it in the cement soil along Madison Avenue.)

"Well, what kind of a title could we give you?" he fumbled. "Something like Consumer Contacts or Customer Relations and Marketing?"

"How about something simple like Account Executive," she suggested, logically enough since that was the spot to be filled.

"But we'd want you to keep on doing the PR too, of course."

"At a combined salary?"

"Well, no. That wouldn't be fair to the other account executives."

Fairness—like beauty—is in the eyes of the beholder. The fact that the little lady was going to be doing two full-time jobs seemed eminently fair to this massive male.

Men (who else?), who do the hiring of account executives usually have one or two wonderful fallback positions when challenged openly about why they aren't hiring a woman. This is especially true of accounts that really cry out for a woman's touch. (The devil will be cutting figure eights after hell freezes over before there's a lady account executive on a big appliance or gas account, although women buy more of both than men.)

In the first place they drag out that old chestnut: A client (a man, of course) would be embarrassed to be entertained by a woman. (!) Victorian sentimentality hangs in there when it can be used to keep a woman out of a good job. With the advent of the credit card—which is remarkably neuter—there's no problem at all in a woman taking a client to lunch, or dinner. There might be some problem entertaining any dirty old men you have on your client list, but there's always some lobby lizard hanging about an account or an agency more than willing to escort a client to a skin flick if his tastes lie in that direction.

Another slight twist on that excuse is: The client just wouldn't feel comfortable in meetings with a woman. The client grew up with one, was taught by others, probably married one and, if long enough in the tooth, might even have some full-grown ones that he's sired. Why a man who has been surrounded by women his entire life should suddenly feel ill at ease across the conference room table from one seems hard to fathom.

Scarce as they are, I've worked with a couple of lady account executives. They were both excellent, buttoned up, and yet easy to work with. They shared one common attribute that is almost unheard of among male account executives: When a work order for a campaign, a TV spot, or just a small space ad came from either one of them, it came complete with all the information and directions a writer needed to complete the job quickly and painlessly. Some of the nicest guys in the business will have you running around from office to office, meeting to meeting, to pick up the facts you need to do the ad. And in this confused treasure hunt, for every straight fact you get you also pick up at least one or two wrong directions.

Probably everyone who lived through the 1965 blackout has his own favorite story about that night. The lights went out all over the East—and stayed out—and a lot of people did the same thing. My night in the dark just happened to involve a lady account executive and her client, a nice guy from the Midwest. They were headed for Penn Station where she was about to catch the train for her home in Princeton, and he was about to return to his room at the Hilton when everything went dark.

At that moment I was taking a nap, completely unaware of what was happening, having had the good sense to go home that day at noon with a headache. When I woke up around 6 p.m. I thought at first that the bulb was dead, then I thought the fuse was blown. I opened the door to the corridor of my barely completed high-rise figuring that the workmen who were constantly under foot had inadvertently spliced two wrong wires together. Only when I looked out over the city did I realize the whole place was blacked out. By then I was sure the Russians were at least as near as the Bronx. My neighbor from one floor below tapped on my door, candle in hand, and explained she was sure she was the one they were after and she wanted company. So by candlelight we opened the bar, and sat down to await the holocaust—with drinks in our hands and fear in our hearts.

We had scarcely tucked into our first nip when the phone came to life. It was my lady account executive—now somewhere on the West Side, with the client still in tow. She wondered if she could spend the night at my place since no trains were pushing off for Princeton in the foreseeable future. "Sure," I said, "if you don't mind the climb up to the seventeenth floor." (For this kind of inconvenience I was paying an arm and a leg!) There was a funny little pause, and then: "I wonder if I could bring Roger (the client). He doesn't feel like climbing all the stairs to his hotel room."

"Listen, if he'd really rather walk all the way across town and then climb seventeen flights, bring him along." It wasn't until halfway through the long, dark night that we all discovered that Roger's room at the Hilton was actually twenty blocks closer to where they'd been when she called—and a half a dozen flights closer to the ground.

So there were going to be four of us for din-din. (Fortunately the stove was gas, not electric.) I peered into my dim and rapidly warming freezer only to find a dozen boxes of melting hors d'oeuvres, a dwindling but still adequate ice cube supply, and a quarter of a pound of chopped steak. Despite all those years of collecting helpful money-saving tips, I was stymied for a way to stretch four ounces of meat—no matter how highly Gristede's had thought of it—to feed four people, two of whom had been climbing stairs for most of the evening and, I imagined, working up sizable appetites. How many bread crumbs can you mix with one hamburger patty?

When the client and the account lady arrived, they were fortunately more thirsty than hungry. We had hardly dented the first fifth when spaghetti and meat sauce crossed my mind. So while we sat in candlelit, shoes-off informality, a pot of spaghetti sauce simmered merrily on the range. We ate around midnight and we were all so well brought up that to this day, I don't know which one of us found the meat in the sauce.

Not knowing the utility companies then as well as we do now, we kept expecting it would be fixed momentarily. Far into the night, and even further into the Scotch, the account lady and I were both ready to call it a night. Two cozy little beds with our names on them were a step away in the next room. But Roger had a long walk and another climb between him and his cot at the Hilton. He was doing his best to keep the conversation going, hoping that at any moment the lights and the elevators would go back on. In practically any other apartment on the island of Manhattan, he could have curled up on the couch and caught a few winks. But my living room's furnished in velvet covered, ornately carved rosewood Victorian chairs and love seats. You could do yourself bodily harm trying to nap on one of them and even sitting on them isn't an unadulterated joy. But you tell a decorator you like Victorian and what does he care—you're only comfortable when you're at someone else's place.

We made an honest effort to stay up all night, but finally had to give in. Roger was sent out to the stairwell and the long dark night. The two of us had slept about an hour when every lamp in the place blazed on and woke us. I ran around the apartment turning off all the lights, and hoping sincerely that the lights had gone on in the Hilton before poor Roger had climbed all those stairs.

A friend of mine joined the select ranks of female account executives via the networks and the media department of her agency. She had left the network where she'd found relative happiness until she got married. At that point, a monthly inquisition by her boss began, no beating around the bush, no euphemisms, but at least once a month: "Well, are you pregnant yet?" If the questioning wasn't bad enough, she realized that she would never get a promotion there, her boss was so sure she was about to reproduce and blow her career. She's now making twice what he'll probably ever make—and in case he's reading this book, she still isn't pregnant.

She was not only the agency's first lady media supervisor and first lady associate media director, but also the first lady account executive on a Procter & Gamble account. You can imagine how much they must have thought of her out in Cincinnati to have overlooked this peculiarity. When I asked her if she'd run into any problems at the agency—beyond the initial shock—she remembered only one: a lady copywriter who was used to having the account man carry her storyboards and luggage for her on all trips to the client. She wasn't too keen about hauling her own things around, and couldn't very well ask the account lovely to do it!

Out in Cincinnati, the reaction to having a lady account man was split: Half of the men prefaced every invitation for dinner with "You must meet my wife" and the other half wouldn't have dreamed of letting her meet the little woman.

In the classic, keep 'em barefoot and pregnant school of thought, the argument is: "I can't have a woman account executive, she'll keep getting pregnant on me and leaving." In this day and age of such sophisticated weaponry against the unconceived, this argument would hardly seem to hold water. But the number of men who are hiding behind it is amazing. The story of a lady account executive I worked with really should lay this chestnut to rest. She was expecting her first child, unbeknownst to those who were working with her every day, but because her doctor had vetoed any travel during her last month, she had had to confide her condition to her immediate superior; no one else in the agency knew. One Friday— facing the usual Manhattan cab shortage—she stood on the Madison Avenue bus all the way home, had four couples in to a dinner she prepared herself and, after the brandy had been served, invited a couple of the guests to join her and her husband on a trip to the hospital. Just before midnight her first child was born, much to the surprise and delight of everyone on her account, including the management head man. He was a marvelous Edwardian type who, had he known she was with child, would probably have had her home on a chaise with weak tea and toast for four months before the blessed event.

The account lady's second son was also born on a Friday earlier on in the day, but since it was the Friday of the long Thanksgiving week end, the most punctilious could scarcely fault her. Despite all the male arguments against women as account executives, this particular lady account executive had done something no man could have done: She actually produced two little consumers for her client, who was very big in baby food.

CHAPTER V

It Worked for Eve

Ever since Eve sold an apple for the highest price on record, women have been using sex to make sales. With it they have sold everything from empires to deodorants. Some of them have even been known to barter it for everything from a mess of pottage at Le Grenouille to that four-letter word, wife, attached to their credentials. With their outrageous success in this area, it is not surprising to find so many of them practicing their wiles in the money-green halls of advertising.

Because so many have had to use their feminine guile to obtain what small measure of recognition they've managed, you will find very few women's lib members prowling Madison Avenue. The ladies of advertising honestly feel they've found a better way. Sure, you'll find a few who resent the double standard, but it is mostly in connection with equal pay for equal work. Stop manning the barricades, men. They're not after a key to the executive washroom—they just want their fair share of the pension plan. The inequities here are not to be believed.

Had I been a man, working for the same length of time and at the same salary, at the last agency I worked in, I'd have walked off with enough loot to retire happily to some un-combed beach. But because women had to be older to get into the plan, had to stay longer to be eligible, and then were not eligible for as big a slice, I have been forced to pick up my poison pen to support myself. No matter how stacked you were, no matter how bright your copy, and no matter how enchanting the chairman of the board found you, that's the way it worked—no exceptions. It's all part of the syndrome that's had women being paid off in nontaxable ways every since Eve's deal with the apple backfired.

Despite the inequities, there are still few rumblings from the ladies of the Avenue. They have become such experts at using their wiles to get their ways, they're convinced there's no need to resort to the whip. A girl doesn't have to use sex to get ahead, but if nature was more generous with your endowments below the neck than above, you needn't consider it a handicap. There are always enough people around who can write or think or whatever is called for to carry a few lovelies who can't.

I once worked at an agency where we had a tall beautiful blonde copy cub. Copy cub is a term used to cover the fact that she's barely making beans, and is also a dodge the creative director uses when Personnel asks him how come he hired a copywriter whose only experience has been acting in summer stock. Anyhow, this copy cub had trouble locating the letters on the typewriter keys and she didn't want to wear glasses because her agent thought it would spoil her image. But she had legs that were still going where most girls had waists, and so she did just fine.

Before you break something jumping to any conclusions, this does not mean all lady copywriters—or even most of them—spend their time in some guy's bed. I'm not saying it isn't done, I'm just saying it isn't done by everyone. A clever girl can use feminine wiles without resorting to anything below the belt—or even below her neck.

One of the most successful ladies ever in advertising was a highly respected executive vice president of one of the country's largest advertising agencies when most women's lib members were picking up whatever they could at their mother's knee. She was also one of the most physically unattractive females you would want to lay your eyes on. Short, dumpy and dark with outcroppings of hair where there was really no need for them, but you should have seen her work the old magic. I've seen board rooms filled with marketing giants practically begging her to take on their accounts.

Her shtick was that she was earth mother and she understood the Frowzy Little Housewife better than anyone else. She had little panels of Frowzy Little Housewife types long before anyone else ever thought of consumer research. She never made a move or suggestion without checking out her panel of FLHs. Now I'm not saying that you have to be dumpy and hirsute to rap with a FLH, but it sure doesn't get in your way. You see, she knew better than any leggy, golden-tressed lovely ever could about just how much fun was missing from the life of the average FLH. So she told them how they could be creative, how to have fun with her products. That dumpy little lady probably sold more soap, more soup, more cake mixes, and God knows what else, than any other single human on earth.

When she got even longer in the tooth, she packaged herself as grandmotherly, and everything she pitched was grandmother good. Now even in today's climate where all your hangups can be traced to your mother, even psychiatrists don't murmur a word against grandmothers!

When that grandmotherly good lady was a power at her agency, it was the second largest one in the country. She's gone

44

now—and the agency might *still* be second if she were there now.

But, of course, anyone big enough to reach the water cooler knows that ladies like that are the exception . . . right? So before any of the male chauvinists in the crowd start breathing heavily, let's keep in mind two points. First: Sex, if it's to be at all profitable, involves two consenting adults and in almost all cases, one of them is male. And second: There isn't a male in the world who doesn't use sex whenever he can. And I'm not talking about the most obvious cases of what is euphemistically called client entertainment. Very few of those ladies of the evening are in anyway else connected with the ad game. But don't despise advertising for this kind of thing. If you were selling nuts to the biggest nut and bolt user in the country, and he were in town for a little fun, you know you'd find him a playmate. That's really all those account men at agencies are doing. They're just following to the letter that title on the door: "A full service agency." It's part of the game. It's just that four blocks west of Madison they call it by its generic name, pimping.

Bristol Myers, when I was shilling for one of their deodorants, subscribed to a research service which periodically ran around peeking into medicine chests and kitchen cabinets. They felt that the true test of a commercial was not what a consumer said she remembered about the commercial or what she could parrot back to you about the product, but whether or not it moved her enough to go out and buy the product.

It always struck me as a pretty clever—and accurate—way to judge your advertising. Every few months, they'd report back to Bristol Myers what they'd discovered in their latest chest and cabinet snoop, and all the agencies that handled BM accounts would be invited over to hear the news—good or bad. The head of this research outfit had a fondness for charts, and a heavy German accent. And you always knew as soon as you walked into the conference room whether the news was going to be good or bad. There was always this one infallible barometer: If the good doctor was there to drop bad news, his zoftig assistant who did a lot of chart shuffling wore a very low cut decolletage; the lower her neckline, the worse the news. And if she did a lot of pencil dropping and stooping before the meeting got under way, at least one agency and maybe all of them would be in for real trouble.

For all those guys who've come back from presentations or pitches where some lovely carried the day muttering that the account probably changed hands in bed, here's a true story to restore your faith in the natural goodness of things.

In one agency, which'll have to remain nameless, there was a little guy with a lot of clout who came to power not in the usual ways. On his feet or his seat he'd never made over $7,500 a year. He used to brag about this to his friends. And since the story is now in the public domain, right away you can see how perceptive he was in choosing his friends. Anyhow, there he was—we'll call him Max—bottoming out on the income charts out West when all of a sudden he beds and weds a lovely whose daddy was very big on the boards of a really big brokerage house and a really big department store.

It should come as no surprise to anyone over the age of consent that our hero soon found himself head of his very own agency with a big brokerage house and a big department store account. So prestigious were these two accounts that they attracted others, and caught the eye of a silver-haired NY agency head who was to retire in a year or two and wanted to dispose of his big chunk of agency stock. He slips Max the stock, the two agencies merge, and before the ink on the deal has dried, Max is winging in from the West anxious to make it big in our town.

As a large share holder in this agency, he carries considerable clout. Enough to force his way down the throats of the rest of the workers and the surprised silver fox into an earlier-than-planned retirement.

The little lovely who has made him what he is today is left back in the Golden West with a small child and an even smaller settlement. He arrives unencumbered to take up his role as playboy of the month, accompanied only by his secretary.

For the benefit of all *Ladies' Home Journal* loyalists who like their endings sweet, let me add that his better side finally surfaced and he has recently made an honest woman of his loyal secretary. Now the two of them sit in their duplex looking down on all those people who think you need brains to make it in advertising.

Lovers of the classics, I'm sure, would much prefer stories of lovelies who've made it to the top on their backs. The bar car to Darien has echoed with these apocryphal tales for so many years that they hardly bear repeating. But there's something so basically satisfying in the O'Henry ending of *this* little morality tale I can't resist it.

At a small agency making it mostly with booze and fashion accounts, there was an executive vice president who was long on looks, but short on those characteristics that make the English such good sports on the playing field. A lady account executive at the same shop was doing a super job running a good-sized piece of drug business when she fell for Mr. Charm. I mean she really cared. But after a roll or two, Mr. Charm decided he preferred someone longer of limb and shorter in tooth and so he turned to the receptionist (supposedly the best-looking in the city). The lady account executive did all the sulky things dropped women have been doing since time began. Mr.

Charm figured he'd give her something else to complain about so he demoted her from the big drug account to a birdseed account. But he hadn't figured on her charm overcoming her sulks, and she made such a hit with the birdseed folks, the client hired her to be on his team. And the first morning she's on the other side of the conference table, she gets on the horn to Mr. Charm back at the agency and tells him she's taking her birdseed to another agency!

Lest any young lovely be tempted by the preceding morality tale to go forth and do likewise, this might be as good a place as any for Barbara's rules. Barbara's a copywriter who has put together an eminently sensible rating system for copywriters thinking of having an affair:

Category	Rating	Reason
Account Executive	Good	Although considered the natural enemy of the copywriter, there is a certain fascination in consorting with the enemy.
Art Director	Fair	A common choice, but carrying with it the tedium of replaying the argument in bed that they have in the office: Who's on top?
Man on the way up	Poor	Asking for future trouble. If he ends up working for you, then what do you do? If you end up working for him, then what don't you do?
Agency Biggie	Excellent	Nice work if you can get it, and if you do, get something for it—like stock.
Client	Unfair	Very dangerous. Remember, when the affair ends, and they invariably do, they never fire the client.

Before involving yourself in any intra-office alliances, it might be well to commit these rules to memory.

But like all rules, they were meant to be broken, as many copywriters can attest to. When a friend of mine took on the job as second in command of the creative department at a smallish agency here in New York, he was told by the creative director that he could pretty much have his way in hiring and firing with one exception. *She* was not to be tampered with, nor was her job to be threatened.

After a few weeks there, he realized that *she* was the weakest link in the creative chain, and he asked his boss what gave her such security. His boss had to admit he wasn't quite sure, but her legendary security had been passed on to him when he had joined the agency some time before. Determined to discover her hold, the two of them went through her desk rather carefully during one of her leisurely two-hour lunches and discovered her security blanket. It was a rather carefully annotated diary, listing time, place, and general topics discussed during her assignations with a famous beer baron who had one of his smaller brands at that agency. The bittersweet footnote to this tale of well-requited love was that the beer baron had long since pulled his account out of that agency, but the legend and the lovely had lived on. It's good to keep in mind that women in love have memories that would put an elephant to shame.

No need to get bogged down here on whether or not it's fair or right that women use sex to get ahead. It's as fair as all those generations of men who have always used a woman's sex to keep her underpaid, underprivileged and under their thumbs. For every woman who's making it *because* of her sex, five—maybe six—million women are being held back because of it.

Despite all this, or maybe because of it, the fairer sex hasn't always been universally fair. There was a sweet young Southern belle at Ogilvy once who married another writer there. Like a lot of other agencies who fear nepotism (or worse), they had a rule against relatives working in the same office. It'll undoubtedly please the women's lib members in the crowd to hear that, contrary to tradition, it was not little Nell who was locked out in the cold. She stayed on, and he was out on the street. It would be a prettier tale by far if I didn't have to add that shortly after losing his job through his marriage, he lost his wife through a divorce.

Regardless of what you've heard or overheard, for every gal who makes it in bed, there are hundreds who make it with their heads. You don't hear about them because who's interested in a brainy broad? But the legend of dumb girl who makes it to the top using only her body has become so widespread that even some people who should know better, fall for it.

There was a very bright, sort of pretty girl working as a secretary in the creative department of one of the top ten agencies a few years back. She was fresh from the West and determined to make it to the top. She grew up on the same Ginger Roger movies that I did. Who can blame her? She was as bright as they come and she'd have made it sooner or later with her writing. But she started believing those stories you hear around the water cooler. So she decided to speed things up by divorcing her art director husband and started collecting vice presidents. She was twenty-five then and, like I said, she was just sort of pretty, but she really radiated sex. Men felt her move into a room before they even saw her. It was something another woman might not notice, but no man ever missed it. So the path through the percales to success seemed a natural.

She moved from a job as a $115 per week secretary to one as

a $15,000 per year writer by walking four blocks east with some borrowed proofs and some great word of mouth from her current vice president. Now everybody in the business knows her because she's slept her way around half the agencies in town. But somewhere along the road to the big dollars a sad thing happened to her: She really lost all confidence in herself as a writer. And at one time she was one helluva good writer. She could have easily held her own or even continued moving up just with her typewriter, but she started believing her own PR and she became convinced herself that she'd only made it because she'd done so much sleeping around.

Her first grey hair became a real threat to her career. And because she felt so damned insecure, she began drinking more than was really necessary. And so to the first few grey hairs you can now add puffy eyes and the beginning of that bloated look. Every time she looked in the mirror, she could see her career going down the drain. To assuage her insecurities, she began collecting husbands. She didn't really care whether they were someone else's or not, just as long as they eventually became hers. She became a real marriage junkie. Now legally entitled to more last names than BBDO, she's unable to find a job as a copywriter. She might not have made it to forty grand a year quite so fast if she'd done it strictly with her writing, but she'd never have made it down so fast either.

The next time you meet a sweet young thing who lowers her eyes demurely and admits she's a copywriter, there's no law says you *have* to ask her, "How come a nice girl like you wants to get mixed up in that?" Remember, she might just be tucking those dimpled knees under a typewriter table every morning and writing the best advertising you've ever seen. If you're wondering why—with so many lovelies thinking their way to the top—there are so many stories about the ones who've made it on their backs, remember: It's a lot easier for some

51

guy to justify losing his headline, his campaign, or his account to a girl if he can claim she won by using her sex. Listen, if I had a nickel for every sour grape that was chewed the morning they announced that Mary Wells walked off with the Braniff account, I could buy the biggest agency in New York. You must have heard the boys crushing all those sour grapes yourself. Lines like: "You can't persuade a guy to paint his planes pink using just logic."

What I have never understood was the reasoning behind the news release announcing the subsequent departure of Braniff from WRG and the arrival of T.W.A. No excuse was needed from the WRG shareholders' point of view. There was never a contest between those two widely disparate budgets. But the Braniff shareholders were given the excuse that there was a "conflict of interests" when the president of a company shares bed and name with the president of the airline's agency. What a perfectly rotten view of marriage they must have, if they don't mind that same president of their airline sharing bed and name with the president of a competitor's agency!

CHAPTER VI

Between a Nun and a Whore

If you think a Jewish mother has high standards when she's choosing an acceptable wife for her son the doctor, you should be around when a client is picking an agency to represent his product. The search for this ideal can be as endless as Diogenes' quest for an honest man. Or it can be as quick and simple a thing as a flash of rapport in the cozy intimacy of a cocktail lounge or the even cozier intimacy of a double bed. Sure, it happens, but despite what a lot of clients' wives suspect, it doesn't happen *that* often. It's too crucial a decision to be made in the feathers. Just how important it is to have the *right* image for your product or the *right* spokesman or woman has been proven over and over.

Probably the best known example of this is the Marlboro Man. The Philip Morris people were trying to boost the sales of a languishing brand which because of its unusually long length—unusual in those days at least—seemed to appeal almost exclusively to women (who are a notoriously smaller market for cigarettes than men). Assuming, and in this case they were quite right, that it was their image and not necessarily their taste that appealed to the ladies, they did an about-face, took Greeley's advice, and went West for their new image. The tall, tattooed cowboy was about as far as you can get from a feminine image and it worked wonders for the brand. Philip Morris rode right along with the Marlboro Man to a fantastic gain in sales. Moved from the bottom of the heap right to the top!

Don't think that little experience didn't teach a lot of people about the importance of the people you show using your product. Months before the government finally decided to ban all cigarette advertising from the tube, they started clamping down on the kinds of people you could show in cigarette spots. First, they said you had to eliminate all sports figures—might have too big an influence on the kids. Then they decided you couldn't show smokers who looked under twenty-five. And just before they blew the final whistle, they decided you couldn't show people really enjoying themselves. As the decrees started piling in with every fresh wind from Washington, one big ciggie exec said that what they really needed in the way of casting for their spots was the Mona Lisa with a cigar in her mouth.

The cigarette people aren't the only ones who can change your mind about a product by flashing a new image on the tiny screen. How many men—or women—ever thought of shaving as an act fraught with all kinds of sexual connotations? Very few, until that blond Scandinavian lovely with the unforgettable accent started urging men to take it off, take it all off with Noxzema.

Doing an about-face on your image the way Marlboro and Noxzema did is the last thing most companies want to do. Either they want to stick with the image they've had for years, maybe updating it a bit, or else they feel they have no clear image in the consumers' eyes and are anxious to establish one.

At BBDO I was involved in updating the Betty Crocker image. For years Adelaide Hawley had been the voice of Betty

Crocker on radio. When General Mills moved into TV, Adelaide appeared in many of their commercials. Competent as she was as a personification of Betty Crocker, there was some feeling out in Minneapolis that perhaps they should have a younger, more modern Betty Crocker. And so the search began.

I can't tell you how many Betty Crocker hopefuls were screen-tested and rejected. It wasn't an easy task to find someone who filled the physical requirements of half a dozen General Mills executives as the girl of their dreams in the same body with someone who looked like she knew her way around the kitchen even better than your mother did. But for a client that size, you try. I mean you *really* try. I think every pretty girl in New York who could boil water was screened. We had several real possibilities. At least we thought we did. They'd pass muster with the first two or three levels of flour executives, but every time we thought we were about to get the OK to sign one up and start making her a household face, somebody up there started to get cold feet.

They were worried out of their minds that women would lose their faith in Betty Crocker if there was an obvious switch in characters. There was someone very high up in the pecking order out there in Minnesota who felt a little like the Pope might feel about a seminarian suggesting that the Sistine Chapel might be more relevant if they retouched God's beard.

No exaggeration, these big-time marketing types were scared to death they'd blow the BC mystique. Now maybe Betty Crocker does not feature big in your list of culture heroines, but you better believe that the little woman who hung over her stove every afternoon watching her cakes rise through her see-through oven door, hung just as heavily on every word that Betty Crocker said. And if you think Virginia was having trouble adjusting to a world without Santa Claus, you can

55

imagine how tough things would be out in Flourland if all those millions of women had their belief in Betty Crocker blown.

Nobody out there wanted to be nailed as the guy who killed Betty Crocker. They had a good thing going and they knew it. They had a whole staff of little ladies who spent their working days just answering letters addressed to Betty Crocker. And I mean these were real answers to real letters; none of this form letter, computer-signed stuff. What kind of a form letter could you write that would give advice on things as diverse as falling soufflés and failing marriages? Every single letter addressed to Betty Crocker got a careful reading and a thoughtful answer.

Eventually it was a search that failed. But before the agency and the client threw in the towel, we had put more women in aprons and on television than all the Pillsbury Bake-offs will ever do!

Probably the easiest image to translate to TV was the Gerber one. Long before I took over their TV problems, they had wisely decided not to put a Mrs. Gerber on the air. A couple of generations of mothers had raised babies on the advice they'd gleaned from Mrs. Gerber's sage words on baby care which were featured in Gerber print advertising for years. Long before Dr. Spock began telling us all how to raise an alienated, undisciplined generation, women were learning how to raise healthy, happy babies from Mrs. Gerber. And it's interesting historically to note that all this wonderful advice through all those years came from the typewriter of Dorrie O'Halloran who never had a baby in her life.

Unlike Betty Crocker, there was a real Mrs. Gerber. That little picture that appeared in the ads was of the real Mrs. Dan Gerber. When you realize that the whole business was started back in the 1920's when Dan Gerber, a young father at the time, told his wife there must be a better way to get baby food than standing over a hot sieve for hours, you've got to realize you're not going to be able to pass Mrs. Gerber off as any mini-skirted mother with all the makeup and lighting tricks known to the trade.

As the number one baby food company in the country, Gerber had no image problems to correct with TV. They just wanted to go on being associated in everyone's mind as the big name in little ones' foods. You couldn't have asked for an easier job. The only award I ever got was for a Gerber TV commercial. But how can you go wrong—showing little babies looking adorable and cuddly and well cared for? Who could hate a company who said "Babies are our business, our only business"? Their shtick was as sacred as motherhood, before the sociologists discovered we were breeding ourselves into a real mess.

And if you think Betty Crocker got a lot of mail, you should have hung around the Gerber mailbox. Mothers just seemed to want to share the problems and joys of their babies with Mrs. Gerber, mother of five, grandmother of eleven. Almost every third letter contained a baby picture and the invariable question, "Don't you think my baby looks like the Gerber Baby?" With empathy like that, you just don't mess around. And that's why there's never been a swinging Mother Gerber on the screen.

With all those mothers out there thinking their babies look like the Gerber Baby, you have to be careful picking the little stars for your commercials. The choice you're offered is enormous. As soon as word went out through the model agencies that Gerber was about to make a commercial, the reception room at D'Arcy filled up with babies like the nurseries at the New York hospitals nine months after the blackout. On top of all the babies the agencies sent, we also had to deal with the babies of the account man's neighbors and friends, the mail-boys' babies, the receptionist's godchild, etc. Turns out everybody in town seems to be shilling for some tot. Suddenly everybody's got a baby to push. But it's no wonder, really. With the SAG contracts what they are today, any baby who appears in a network TV commercial while he's in diapers can be sure of enough loot to see him through college when he's in long pants.

Fortunately all babies are adorable, so it's no problem finding one. All you really have to look for is one that's got a fairly happy view of life and doesn't leak too much from either end. But even with babies, a determined producer can goof. One script I wrote called for a baby brother and his older sister. I had in mind a little girl about two or three. I hadn't been in on the casting, and so it came as a bit of a shock to walk onto the set the morning of the shooting and find big sister a toddler of about one year and baby brother a lad of about six months. I mumbled something about having had an older woman in mind for the lead, and just prayed that nobody else would spot the inconsistency. Any mother who had a twelve-month-old daughter and a six-month-old son belonged in the AMA Journal, not in the supermarket picking up baby food!

When you realize the amount of money at stake, it's not surprising that TV mothers are even worse than stage mothers. But I think the honors for being a pushy mother have to go to the one whose kid was being considered for a spaghetti spot. The kid looked just right—tousled blond hair, big grin, and lots of freckles. (On TV you don't have to be Italian to love spaghetti!) But there was just this one little problem: The client had his heart set on having a kid with one front tooth missing, and this kid still had all his baby teeth. Would you believe that mother offered to take the kid's tooth out if he got the job?

The really fortunate company has a built-in image in the

person of someone in the company. But how many companies can be as lucky as the fried chicken chain owned by old Colonel Saunders with his white linen suits and his flowing mane? Sometimes, though, a company's image literally just walks into the agency right off the street. That was the case when the representative of Schweppes Ltd., briefcase in hand, distinguished goatee bristling Britishly, appeared at Ogilvy for an early meeting on the advertising to introduce the elixir to the colonies. The receptionist, a lovely girl but no whiz at remembering names, phoned the man who was expecting him and announced quite succinctly, "The man from Schweppes is here." She was quite right.

Cosmetic companies are notorious for having a hard time putting their finger on the girl of their dreams; each cosmetic mogul sees his consumer from a very subjective viewpoint. A friend of mine, who was part of the search team for the Rubinstein girl, spent some of the happiest hours of his life screen-testing an almost endless series of young lovelies. The few who made it past the first echelon of the Rubinstein staff just never seemed to make it past the second.

You can get your daughter into the best finishing school in the country with fewer screening interviews than you need to get her into a network television commercial—especially when there are several levels of authority. The girl who appeals to the callow, young, assistant brand manager, may cut no ice at all with his middle-aged superiors. The more layers of responsibility on the client side, the more opinions you're going to run into on just what the company's image or spokeswoman should look like. So you figure when you're dealing with a company like Revlon where only one man's vote really counts, you've got it licked, right? Wrong.

Back when TV was a new toy, Revlon was one of the first cosmetic companies to use the new medium. That was back

59

when commercials were live like the shows. On *The $64,000 Question*, one of the products we were peddling between questions and visits to the isolation booth was a hair spray that was to return romance to the boudoir by ending nightly pin-ups.

We needed at least two models for every commercial. A "before" girl with her hair up in pincurls, and an "after" girl with her hair all carefully combed out. Now, while you want your "after" girl to look a lot better than your "before" girl, you have to realize that the folks out in videoland aren't going to buy a ringer for Miss America playing "after" and a Phyllis Diller look-alike playing "before." It proved so difficult to find a lovely who wasn't really grotesque looking in a headful of pins, we settled on the only one we could find and used her as the "before" girl week in and week out. Week in and week out, that is, until she really let her hair down for a photographer and appeared centerfold as the Playmate of the Month.

Every week the casting director at BBDO had to come up with a lovely who would come up to the client's fluctuating standards. Second-guessing his mercurial moods was driving the casting director up the walls. After a rather less than successful meeting, he returned to the agency and made one of those classic statements about the whimsicality of clients' ways. Throwing down a bunch of glossies on his desk, he slumped into his chair and said, "Who can please that guy? One week he wants a nun and the next week he wants a whore."

But casting isn't all work and no play. A friend of mine spent a recent afternoon—on company time—standing in for the female lead while they screen-tested Italian lover types for a Campbell soup commercial. Afternoons like that, she claims, make up for a lot of the insecurities of the business.

Almost every girl who comes in for an audition has in her book at least one or two pictures of herself in a bathing suit.

Very few male models ever do. It usually doesn't matter, but when you're casting for a man who has to appear in a shower, you've got to find someone who looks good, at least from the waist up, in his skin. I remember we'd picked one man who had looked just great in his pictures. You know, broad shoulders, trim waist, slim hips, what every girl dreams of, the whole bit. So you can imagine what a shock it was to all of us when he appeared on the set all ready to lather up, with a thick growth of hair not only on his chest but on his back, too. I thought the guys from Suds City were going to faint. After a quick consultation, the poor agency producer got tapped for the job of telling our star he'd have to shave his chest if he was going to share the screen with a bar of Zest.

"I really hated to have to do that," Paul said, after the model left for his second shave that morning. "How's his wife going to feel about this tonight?"

"Forget tonight," I told him. "How's she going to feel when all that stubble starts to grow in?"

CHAPTER VII

"Fly with the Ones Who Gunned Your Sons"

To this day, Tim's wife probably thinks he spent five days in Germany with Sidney, not me. It had all been arranged that way, but at the last minute Sid couldn't go. In a copy department the size of ours, they had to take what they could find. I happened to be the only writer with a valid passport and vaccination certificate as well as no entangling alliances to prevent my going. The purpose of the trip was to come up with some fresh approaches to Lufthansa advertising.

I suppose almost anyone's first reaction to such an assignment is to come up with some smart-ass remark like "Fly with the ones who gunned your sons" and, of course, I did. Listen, I might not have fought in World War II, but I'll match my attendance record at war movies with anybody's. The Luftwaffe always had the bad guys, and this client's name smacked too close to that for comfort or easy imaging. (I always thought they'd be better off advertising themselves as the German-American airline, and now they are.)

With the possible exception of the Japan Airlines copywriter, I figure I'd lucked into one of the bigger challenges of the year. At least the Luftwaffe wasn't notorious for its kamikaze pilots. I felt that had to be a little reassuring to a potential passenger. When you get an assignment like this, you grasp at straws.

Tim and I both had one thing going for us: We were Americans with Irish names. Now, Ireland is one of the few garden spots in Europe that Germany never made a grab for, and the Irish, ever interested in exotic native customs, have always been fascinated by the way Germans work. Not that they'd care to join them in it, thank you, but it's a fascinating thing to watch; in Shannon, I've seen Irishmen actually leave their drinking (no small sacrifice in that climate) to go down the road to watch the Germans working. So right away we were points ahead of another agency's creative team who had recently done the see and tell tour. Like I said, on a tour like this you start out grasping at straws.

I had never written a word on the account, nor had I met any of the Lufthansa New York personnel, and I had only the usual prejudices against the airline based on a total lack of experience with them. I also had only the usual fears about flying, having always felt that the most dangerous part of any trip is getting to the airport. Driving with Tim merely confirmed this belief.

Obviously, anyone who saw our tickets realized we had some connection with the airline since they were freebies. But we did not go out of our way to make known our identities as agency finks. We hoped to see the airline the way the average American tourist sees it. With this particular airline—as their present advertising indicates—it is the average American businessman more than the tourist who gets to see much of Lufthansa.

The flight over was uneventful and pleasant, with the service surprisingly smooth considering they were operating a fully loaded plane. I sat next to an American woman who was on her way to Rome by way of Frankfurt! She was traveling this circuitous route because her husband was a German-American. (Despite all you hear about the Mafia and the Irish pols, the German-Americans are the largest ethnic group in this country. You could run an airline just flying them back and forth.) My seatmate's husband had insisted that she fly Lufthansa—he had that much loyalty or pride or whatever. But he also had enough superstition or whatever to insist that they travel on different flights. People do funny things when they're six miles up.

Our get-acquainted tour began in Frankfurt where we stayed at an Intercontinental Hotel that looked like Intercontinentals the world over: very tall, very new, very efficient. It's located directly on the Main River which made up a bit for the lack of gemütlich. I guess I'd been brought up on too many war movies equating the German imperial eagle with Nazi Germany, and in my mind it sort of was intertwined with the swastika. This is a notion you must rid yourself of if you are to enjoy any time in Germany at all. The German imperial eagle symbol is left over from far happier and far grander days. And it was on everything at the hotel from the cocktail napkins to the shower curtains and bath mats. It took a little adjusting to, but it was just the first of several quickie adjustments my mind had to make. We were there for a five-day business trip, but before it was over I had decided to take some time and do a little touring on my own before returning to New York. That's how much my mind had adjusted.

Tim insisted we'd never get the feel of the country if we stayed hermetically sealed in the Intercontinental's glass tower, so that night we took off on our own, crossed the river into what looked like a strictly residential neighborhood, and found a marvelous little restaurant in one of the houses. Lots of simple but good food, and Tim's first encounter with German beer. It was to become one of the great relationships of the twentieth century. Before our five days of orientation were over, Tim spent an evening in Heidelberg, bending elbows with the students who consider themselves the ultimate beer quaffers. Tim not only held his own, but set some records that I'm sure will stand through generations of Germans to come. He claims it took an Irish-American to show them how to drink. It took him all night, but he showed them.

Meanwhile, back at the hangar in Frankfurt the next day, we were really getting the inside story on how to run an airline. We toured the in-cabin personnel training facilities where the stewards and stewardesses practiced in classrooms and a giant cutaway airliner cabin. The men and women who run this facility—like all Lufthansa personnel—are deeply aware of their image problem. And they are going about trying to soften their image with the same efficiency and determination that they go about everything else. If it doesn't always come off, it's not because they haven't tried or aren't trying, but rather because friendliness and warmth are just not the kind of things you can teach in a classroom. Whether they'd ever admit it or not, they'd give half their fleet, I'm sure, to have their stewardesses rap with passengers the way those lilting-voiced girls on Aer Lingus do. This training school at that time was ten years old and graduating one thousand stewardesses each year; of these three hundred were new and the others were taking refresher courses.

Tim and I must have met close to half a hundred executives and line employees on our little tour, from student pilots and chefs to members of the board of directors. A cross section of people like that is bound to have a tremendous range of personal feelings and attitudes about Americans and things American. But to a man, they were all agreed on one thing: the respect which they had for the American aircraft industry. It was nothing short of worshipful—and from a country that takes no small pride in its industrial know-how, I found that attitude nothing short of amazing. Having been away from the account so long now, I can't guarantee whether it worked out this way, but in 1966 they planned to be an all-Boeing airline by 1970. Lufthansa had introduced the 727 to Europe and was also the first foreign line to fly the 747s.

Also, to a man they are sure their reputation for meticulous care and attention to detail is established. In all their talks with Tim and me they repeatedly emphasized the need to present themselves as a friendly airline of international scope. At the time of our trip, they were dead set against our using the words, "the German Airline", but I notice it in their present advertising, so I guess they are solving some of their hangups.

We spent only an hour or so going through their kitchens in Frankfurt, but you could easily spend a day there. It's the largest in Europe with over seven hundred people in the catering department, including one hundred chefs who prepare ten thousand meals a day. In this kitchen, they also prepare food for twenty-five other airlines. Even here they're as proud of their innovations as they are of their efficiency: They were the first airline to brew coffee on board, the first to carry a real chef aboard for first class service, and they have devised a way of making fresh French fries on board that doesn't involve splattering anyone with hot fat or just heating cold potatoes. They also have devised a way to boil eggs without using water. Maybe it's not the kind of thing that makes you fly an airline, but it is indicative of the thoroughness that shows itself in every phase of their operation.

At the time of our tour, they had recently introduced their "Farmer Service": red checked napkins, wooden plates, and a keg of beer tapped on board. It was designed to give passengers who usually only saw big German cities a taste of the German countryside by emulating a country inn in the sky. It was also part of an attempt to lure more tourists onto their flights; businessmen they have by the planeloads. An American businessman I met on a cruise down the Rhine told me that most businessmen consider it a matter of form to fly at least one way on transatlantic trips with the airline of the country they're doing business with.

Practically at a dead run, we were led through their cargo handling operation in Frankfurt, naturally the biggest and most efficient in Europe. They'd one man there whose only assignment was to see that animals in transit got the proper food and care. The afternoon we dashed through the place there was crated wildlife from Africa and India on its way to zoos in Europe and America, as well as a fairly cosmopolitan crowd of domesticated pets, including a group that had reproduced in transit. (Talk about a friendly airline!)

We were given a slightly slower paced tour of the maintenance operation in Frankfurt. Here's where their fanatic attention to detail really shows. They put twenty-one man hours of maintenance behind every hour of flight which costs $250 per flight hour. The annual overhaul of a jet takes twenty thousand man hours and requires a two-week grounding of the plane. Despite all this, or maybe because of it, Lufthansa had at that time the highest utilization of aircraft rate, twelve to thirteen flight hours per plane a day.

The final facility we were to tour in Frankfurt was a flight training center where pilots who are switching from one kind of plane to another get their instruction. Lufthansa also maintains a similar operation in Tucson, Arizona. At these training centers, pilots, copilots, and their engineers train together as teams. And it is at these bases that a Lufthansa pilot gets a flight check every eight months. Pilots from other airlines are also checked out here. It is not as much of a tower of Babel operation as that would imply, since English is the language of the skies and all pilots must be able to speak it. It is the language they use in communicating with airport control towers all over the world.

Our last night in Frankfurt we were entertained in the home of one of the board members. And Tim and I were not conversant enough in doing business abroad to know what a rare thing this was. He lived in a suburb of Frankfurt that could have passed for any good suburb here in the States, except for the presence on a nearby hill of a marvelously ornate castle that had been built for one of Victoria's daughters.

We had bratwurst grilled over an open coal barbecue on the terrace, and except for the slight accents, we might have been back in Scarsdale. As the shadows grew long in the late twilight, the men began talking of their war experiences. When Tim said he'd been torpedoed in the North Sea, our host said, "Then we must have been swimming companions as boys." In those same waters at about the same time, he'd had a submarine blown out from under him.

Although we were to meet executives of the airline in every city we visited, it was in Frankfurt, their largest installation, where we met most of them. And foremost in the mind of every one of them was an awareness of their image problem. They didn't take it lightly, and they were well aware of the challenge it was for us at the agency. They continually went out of their way to prove that they were doing their best at their end to rectify the problem. For instance, they were trying very hard in all their training to teach their pilots to be in more frequent and friendly contact through the intercom with the passengers. The Lufthansa executives who fly competing airlines all over the world on a regular basis, looking for good ideas to emulate and mistakes to avoid, were all enormously impressed with the amount of small talk that American pilots have with their passengers. At that time they had made little headway, and the communication between Lufthansa pilots and passengers was at the barest minimum.

To be perfectly honest, I have always found chatter from the pilot a mixed blessing. If he is encountering turbulence or sees it coming on his magic instruments, I'd just as soon he'd keep it to himself. I can imagine enough to worry about up there on my own, I don't need his prompting. And pointing out one of the seven wonders of the world visible only from seats on the left-hand side of the plane when I am securely belted into the right-hand side, is only a source of aggravation. However, the Lufthansa executives found it a charming and friendly thing and were determined to force this camaraderie on their pilots, just as they were determined to turn their image around. But it was sticky going and no one would deny it.

At about the time we were touring their installations, the ads were breaking in the first campaign Doyle Dane Bernbach was doing for their international division (a much larger segment of their business than the North American portion D'Arcy was handling). It was a campaign sure to get attention—not all of it favorable. The ads, designed for their shock technique, *were* shocking to the Lufthansa executives. One can hardly blame them and it is a measure of their determination to be considered nice guys that they simply didn't yank the account. Unfortunately I've forgotten the exact headlines, but the gist of the entire series was that the same characteristics that make Germans so unpopular make them great airline mechanics, pilots, etc. You know the approach: You wouldn't want one for a neighbor, but they're great in the hangar and the cockpit. It was a series which fortunately never ran in this country.

Our next stop was Bremen where the pilot training school made us feel we had stepped back into history. There, in a campuslike atmosphere, the new pilots receive their initial training. The ivy on the brick buildings barely concealed the spots where the plaques had been, identifying these same buildings, connected by flower-bordered paths, as the training school of the Luftwaffe during the war.

The head of the school, a tall dark and handsome man, was introduced to us as Herr Vermaarten. (First names are never, but *never,* used with this crowd.) He shook hands with us quite formally, and then before he spoke, he slapped his hand to one leg, and it resounded the way only a wooden leg can. "A present to me from the Americans on my twenty-first birthday," he said, sitting down awkwardly. It was an opener that was hard to top, and neither of us tried. The shoe was definitely on the other foot at this point, and an artificial one at that. It was also a far cry from the "swimming companions" remark of our host the previous evening.

Herr Vermaarten gave us a quick history of the Bremen facility, pointing out before we could ask, that although there *had* been Luftwaffe pilots flying for Lufthansa, most of them had been phased out because of age. The school had been started in 1956 with thirty students and ten years later had two hundred pilots in training. By now they should have four hundred or more.

Pilot training in Germany had been pretty much limited to an elite who could afford the tuition which was sizable, but at that time they were just beginning to bring in some scholarship students. It's a far cry from the on-the-job training we're used to in this country. The washout rate at Bremen is 6 per cent as opposed to the BOAC rate of 25 per cent, the KLM rate of 30 per cent, and the Alitalia rate of 45 per cent. So you see, the efficiency starts early on with this crowd. And it's evidently a hard habit to break, for not one pilot had ever left Lufthansa for another airline at that time.

After our tour of the pilot training base at Bremen, Herr Vermaarten arranged to have us flown to Hamburg by one of the student pilots in one of those teeny trainers that were really not designed to carry people with my fears. We had hardly been airborne five minutes when we flew into the grandmother of all storms—thunder, lightning, hailstones, the works. The hailstones ricocheted off the plane with the sound of machine gun bullets, and the tiny plane bounced around in the sky like a toy in the hands of a spastic child. I couldn't help wondering if perhaps Herr Vermaarten was repaying the Americans for his birthday present. I looked at Tim out of the corner of my terror-stricken eye and saw he was sound asleep.

In Hamburg we saw more pilot training facilities, where the pilots come after two years at Bremen. On the Hamburg flight simulators, pilots from other airlines are also checked. Before a pilot is allowed out in one of the biggies, he must spend fifteen to twenty hours in a simulator. Tim and I each took the controls of the simulator for a short flight. With all the laughing and giggling, I think we theoretically crashed over theoretical Zurich. If you're going to crash, the simulator is the place to do it.

Also in Hamburg are the technical schools where apprentices start after their secondary school graduation. They train for three and a half years before they are allowed to wield a wrench on anything that flies. Most of them live at home and are given free lunches, work clothes, and transportation; foreign students are given a living allowance. Special and separate living quarters have been set up for apprentices from Spain and Italy. As our guide explained, "They cook with garlic, and it wouldn't be fair to those living around them."

The most fascinating place we saw in Hamburg was the maintenance and overhaul facility. At that time Lufthansa had over four thousand specialists in the technical division as opposed to around five hundred captains and co-captains. In Hamburg all overhauling as well as short haul maintenance is done; long haul maintenance is done in Frankfurt. This is the spot where that meticulous German attention to detail is most impressive. As far as the eye can see are rows and rows of what look like library stacks, but are really the tool files. Not only does every tool have a place clearly marked for it in these files, but each tool is examined and signed by an inspector once each month. Here, too, they actually make the tools themselves at a quarter of the price it would cost them to buy them. Sealed emergency kits containing every tool and part necessary for repairing a defective engine are ready to be flown to any place in the world. When a jet is overhauled here, every part gets from ten to twenty baths, then is subjected to four separate checks including fluorescent, molecular structure, and magnetic crack detection. Jet engines all checked and ready to be put in place are on stands at wing height so that a complete jet engine replacement from landing to takeoff takes only four hours. That's another reason Lufthansa planes spend less time on the ground than any other airline's.

A white-coated, distinguished looking type who could have passed muster at a medical center took us on our tour of the maintenance facility. He told us that if he were to find a minute part, smaller even than a thumbnail, lying on the floor of the hangar, he would be able to tell us not only from which type plane it had come, but from exactly where in that plane. I also had the sneaking feeling that if he had found a minute part lying on the floor of that immense building—large enough to handle the overhaul of several big jets at once—heads would roll.

I imagine because of international regulations all airlines must have similar operations and techniques, but I must say I never had a more secure feeling in the air than I did on the flight home. Under the auspices of the airline, I had had answered the question D'Arcy was then posing in its advertising for Lufthansa: "How far can an airline go for you?" And on my own I had discovered Germany is one of the easiest of all European countries for an American to tour. I had met some memorable Germans and some that were just plain hard to forget.

We had a full dress review of the trip when we got back. During it, the management supervisor asked me what was the one single thing I, as a potential passenger on an airline, would find most reassuring. I told him, a pilot who hadn't had a fight with his wife that morning. I was taken off the account almost as quickly as I had been put on it. But it's an account I've always felt a soft spot for.

D'Arcy's swan song campaign, "This year think about Germany, think twice about Germany," even if it had not been picked up for satirization by *Scanlon's* with pictures of German atrocities riding above the headline, has to have been the biggest gaffe of the year. Who was getting his jollies out of it we'll probably never know, but you can bet your thesaurus they could never have sold that slogan to a company with even a passing knowledge of the American idiom. McCann-Erickson is now promoting Lufthansa as "The route of the Red Baron." I hope it's working for them. They deserve a lot better than they were getting.

CHAPTER VIII

One Man's Ink Blot

Right in time for holiday voyeurs last year, Grand Old Parr Scotch came out with what must have been the ad of the year for all the dirty old men in the crowd. Beneath the headline, "There's a right age for everything. In Scotch, it's Grand Old Parr, the deluxe 12-year-old," is a picture of a gentleman of more than mature age in black tie, holding a glass and standing behind a sweet young thing curled up in some furry kind of chair. The little lovely, her face innocent of makeup, her long blonde hair hanging loose below her shoulders, could easily pass for the same age as the Scotch. Now what pops into your mind when you see a setup like this under a line like that is really none of my business. But what popped into my mind evidently popped into quite a few others, too, for the agency that produced the ad found itself on the receiving end of considerable criticism. Naturally they were surprised, shocked, and chagrined that anyone should have so misread their intentions and their ad. According to an agency spokesman, the picture was cropped to fit the ad's space, and in doing the cropping, the girl's left hand—wedding band ablaze—was inadvertently cut off. The agency also said the model was twenty-three years old.

Just how much of the evil in that ad was in the eye of the beholder was brought home loud and clear to me at lunch the other day when another lady of the Avenue and I were listing our nominees for the bad taste of the year award. I mentioned the Scotch ad, and she said she didn't see anything wrong with showing "a father and daughter in an ad, but the girl did seem a bit young to be drinking"! Listen, it not only makes horse racing; that same difference of opinion also makes for a lot of the fun in advertising.

In one case it made for one of the most successful campaigns ever run—a campaign that literally single-handedly built a market that hadn't existed before. It wasn't too long ago when any lady who colored her hair was considered no better than those painted women who plied their trade in the street. If a good woman wanted to change the color of her hair or disguise the grey in it, she took to the back booths at the hairdresser's and there, in hushed tones and behind closed curtains, he worked his evil transformation. One thing you *never* talked about was coloring your hair. Until Shirley Polykoff happened on the scene with her hamisha ways, her Jewish grandmother image, and one of the great lines of all times: "Does she or doesn't she? Only her hairdresser knows for sure." The men in the crowd giggled and tittered a lot and said it was a great line, but of course you couldn't get away with it. Too obvious a double entendre, they all said. All the talk in the world couldn't convince them that it was only in the minds of men that the line meant anything off-color, you should pardon the expression. It was only after a homegrown survey of secretaries and other female innocents that Miss Polykoff was able to convince them.

Whether the girls got it and were too embarrassed to admit it, or whether they missed it entirely, we'll never know. But it's academic now. The line ran, and it turned people's ideas and preconceived notions about haircoloring completely around, built a fantastic market, and made discussing the color you use on your hair as acceptable a topic as the shade you're wearing on your lips.

Like every successful campaign, it was bound to have its imitators. And one of the least successful imitators on record came up with a campaign a few seasons back that managed to offend more people than it persuaded. It was for some hair care product whose brand name mercifully escapes my memory, but the headline keeps ricocheting in the dark recesses of my mind where all things I'd rather forget are stored. Above a picture of a lovely with gorgeous hair, the line ran: "Her husband's in love with her hairdresser." If it didn't manage to offend most of the husbands in the crowd, it most certainly didn't make any points with the hairdressers. One of the problems with introducing sex as a hidden salesman in your ad is that sex, like beauty, is often in the eyes of the beholder. It's hard to know when one man's ad is going to turn into another man's ink blot.

When you're proposing a line like "Does she or doesn't she?" you kind of expect a little resistance from certain quarters. But when you present an ad that to you couldn't possibly offend or excite, and it's turned down as prurient, you're really caught by surprise. It happened to a friend of mine who was working on one of those island accounts that can be such fun when you can grab off a few days of fun in the sun and chalk it up to product research, but can also be such a strain when every ad you present has to be approved by half the government before it can run. Barbara, the writer on this mixed blessing of an account, once told me that every ad had to be OKd right down to the final comma by anywhere from thirty to one hundred islanders, "people who had little to do but drink, gossip, and tear the island's advertising to shreds."

The ad in question (or questionable taste—depending on which side of the hangup you sat) was in trouble not because of its headline, a straightforward enough thing suggesting you might enjoy a visit to this island; it was the picture that turned off one of the MPs. And it was just one girl in a picture that must have included at least a dozen people disporting themselves in the sun and in the water. The picture made you want to grab your towel and sandpail and head for that beach by the next balloon. Unfortunately, the lovely under attack aroused other feelings deep down inside the MP. She was the usual exquisite-looking model, rail thin as they always are, and she was lying in the sun on her beach towel.

By arguing loudly and emotionally enough to sway the rest of the panel, he talked them into killing the ad because the girl was *obviously* on the island only to pick up men, and *obviously* for money at that. The agency people couldn't believe their ears, and asked the livid MP what made him think the girl was doing either of those evil things. He flustered and blustered about her figure (as far from voluptuous as models' figures invariably are), and her costume (the basic bikini in fashion on his beaches for some years then) until finally it came out: It was the size of her beach towel that did it. It was far too large and commodious a beach towel to be carried by anyone interested merely in the sun and surf, according to this keeper of the island mores. A towel like that, he was convinced, was up to no good and meant to be shared. (Now are you beginning to see why so many clients insist that their models always wear wedding rings?) And so, because of one man's hangup about beach towels, a really good ad and a great deal of work went down the drain. It wasn't long after that that the account also went down the drain, and there were few to mourn its loss— with the exception, oddly enough, of the writer on the account. Despite its bad weather, bad food, and lack of nightlife, she had grown inordinately fond of the island. If she ever returns to it, however, she'll have one of the smallest towels on the beach.

It seems hard to believe now, with women disporting themselves on every beach in costumes that would fit neatly into an egg cup, and appearing on the streets and in offices in see-through blouses and an obvious distaste for much in the way of underpinnings, that there was a time when the sight of a female navel was considered far too daring to show in a magazine. It wasn't that long ago, either. Just a year or two before the little anatomically accurate boy dolls were being thrust into the arms of girls too young to even pronounce what they were holding, the editors of *Seventeen* magazine felt that the sight of a navel might be embarrassing or offensive to their teen-age readers. (And if you know any of today's teenagers you know that nothing short of overt sentimentality embarrasses them.) The editorial decision probably would never have been a nuisance to any advertiser, except that it was still in effect long after bikinis were being shown both editorially and in ads in the magazines. And it required a great deal of airbrushing around the midsection of a lot of sweet young things before any summer issue went to bed.

When an advertiser runs a commercial with a sexy dame confiding over her shoulder, in accents soft and tender, that "My men wear English Leather, or they wear nothing at all," it doesn't take an evil mind to get the implication—to be as kind as I can be. Frankly, I found it to be one of the most offensive ads of that year or any other. And I am not one to be finding sexual symbolism lurking behind every mixed metaphor; if anything, I lean in the opposite direction. In fact, years after he had torn around suburbia challenging dirt, I had to have the symbolism of the White Knight explained to me! I still resent the recent school of criticism that is finding deep sexual connotations in all the great old nursery rhymes and fairy tales that generations of uncomplicated Americans grew up on. Anybody who's getting his kicks out of Henny Penny and Jack in the Beanstalk should keep it to himself. At least Portnoy had the decency to take his pleasure behind a closed door. At the risk of appearing old-fashioned, I kind of agree with that great Victorian who said he felt any conduct on the street was acceptable, providing it didn't frighten the horses.

If a little knowledge is a dangerous thing, an unknowledgeable copywriter can be a disaster (or at least a near miss). At BBDO we had a demure young lovely who proved to be too straitlaced for her account's own good. Faced with the challenge of writing an ad for a silverware pattern called "Young Love," she presented her boss with the headline, "Try *Young Love* on Your Table Tonight!"

Even her effort must take second place to two lines which tie for the innocents abroad on Madison Avenue award. Both of them were written by women for women, and were concerned about the importance of keeping small wounds clean. The Y&R offering: "Even little pricks can hurt" and the BBDO entry: "Never neglect the little prick."

But if ignorance of colloquialisms can cause embarrassment, ignorance of the product can be even more painful. A decade ago, a sweet young copywriter who had travelled extensively, but only in this country, Great Britain, and its islands found herself assigned to a large plumbing account. She was to write a pamphlet on a bidet, to her a totally uncomprehensible plumbing fixture. Her homegrown research resulted in a lot of smirks from the men she asked and a sudden departure on the part of the women. Having ascertained that it had its origins in France, she invited a French girl of her acquaintance to dinner and a brief quiz. Naturally she was full of all kinds of facts and lore about the product and, being French, more than willing to share her knowledge, even to the extent of explaining that a considerable portion of the French population had been born owing to a widely held faith in the fixture as a birth control device. Girding her loins, the lovely took to her typewriter, stringing together a suitable string of euphemisms, and presented them proudly to the client. He, in a sudden burst of embarrassment, turned them all down, insisting the fixture was just a cure for hemorrhoids! This one man alone may have slowed down the introduction of the bidet to American bathrooms by as much as ten years.

But sexual scintillation, intended or inadvertent, is not the only faux pas that crops up in advertising. Sometimes a good line goes bad because of the product it's pushing. When Sylvia Dowling was asked for a manageability claim for Halo and came up with the line, "Makes your hair more manageable than he'll ever be" followed by a sensuous little giggle, it seemed a natural. Only problem was, the product couldn't deliver the promise in the line. And another great claim bit the dust.

Sometimes the most innocuous ad in the world backfires merely because it was ill-timed. The classic bad timing for an otherwise OK ad occurred when Pan Am ran an ad for its new 747 service in *The Daily Star* of Beirut on September 8, 1970, just two days after the plane had refueled there before its hijacking and destruction in Cairo. The headline was "How to Catch a 747," and the copy ran in part, "The 747 is the finest specimen in the air. But oddly enough it's becoming just about the easiest to catch. And you won't have to go sneaking up on it if you're in Europe on the way to the USA." It's media scheduling like that that turns copywriters and clients old before their time.

CHAPTER IX

Can't We Make It Habit-Forming?

Despite what you see on your television set, in Adland the battle is not between the good guys and the bad guys; the really big action is between research and marketing departments. The disputed territory is, of course, the marketplace. Marketing men, convinced they know exactly what Mrs. Consumer out there is waiting for, make continual pilgrimages to the ivy-covered research departments asking that just such a widget be developed. Research men on the other hand, the purest, most uncommercial scientists to come down the pike since Arrowsmith, are much more interested in what their little test tubes have produced lately. They dump their latest discoveries at the doorstep of the marketing departments demanding a market be found for them.

Marketing men can't see why the Research and Development boys can't come up with a self-capping toothpaste tube; R&D men can't see why the marketing boys are having trouble selling hashish-flavored haggis; copywriters can't see why they can't come up with a new product that's habit-forming. Out there in Consumerland, the average housewife is still wondering why someone doesn't invent packaging she can open without breaking her nails, her resolution to stop using four-letter words, and the package.

This tendency to permanently encase products as though they were to last until the apocalypse is not new. Early on, at one of those sessions at my mother's knee, I learned that it is humanly and mechanically impossible to open a can of evaporated milk without one of those little metal gadgets that became collector's items back when Lincoln was a boy. (Don't scoff till you've tried it. It is the one can in all the world without that little ridge on top for the can opener to grab hold of.) But women are a long-suffering crowd, and given the proper sell on the product inside, they'll persist in superhuman efforts not only to find the package on the crowded shelves, but to open it and use the contents as well.

But it's the product, not its packaging, that concerns us here, and some of the minor skirmishes in the never-ending war between R&D and marketing. One interesting aside first: The world's largest cosmetic company neatly and profitably avoids all this internecine warfare by only introducing new products that have been carefully thought out by their product development department. These men keep their fingers on the pulse of the market, and by tossing trends and new products into a marvelous computer which adds up potential sales for such products, they come out with pretty buttoned up recommendations. It is only at that point that they approach their test tube boys. You don't introduce a lot of innovations that way, but then again you never introduce a real bomb either.

Any copywriter who spends more than forty-eight hours in the business is inevitably dragged into this battle of the departments. It becomes the writer's problem to find a selling idea that has appeal in the great marketplace for all these unwanted breakthroughs. Having written the introductory advertising which moved a new deodorant, a bath bar, a furniture polish, and a cake mix into first place nationally, I found myself with somewhat of a reputation as a new product maven, so I lucked into what I felt was more than my fair share of these assignments. But they're not all lemons, obviously. The best advertising in the world isn't going to move a loser into the winner's column. Look at the great advertising Piel's ran for so long—and it got them nowhere.

Sometimes, of course, it is not your client's but some other company's R&D department which comes up with a magic ingredient and offers it to you to market. A friend of mine was involved in just such a case. The test tube tyros at Union Carbide came up with a secret ingredient that would turn a liquid into a gel. Knowing what titans Procter & Gamble were in the marketing game, they offered it to them on an exclusive basis for ten years, then geared up to produce masses of this magic ingredient at a healthy profit.

The new product wheels started to grind out in Cincinnati, and like those other well-known wheels, they grind slow but exceeding fine. The magic ingredient was put into a man's hairdressing named Radar. It was really a breakthrough product, an innovation. Maybe the world wasn't waiting breathlessly for it, but then again, it wasn't bored to death with the idea either.

Prospects for having a winner on their hands seemed pretty good when P&G started out in their first test market. Because the product was so innovative, they decided to throw caution to the wind, eschewing slice of life commercials for something a tad racier. The idea was to have a really sexy dame writhing about on a tiger rug, giving the pitch for the product. No sooner had they put this little epic on film and scheduled it to run in the test market cities than they flipped on their TV sets

83

one night and saw a very similar girl lying on a very familiar looking skin, pitching a competitive hair groomer, and this one in national distribution.

So that test went down the drain and it was back to the drawing boards to come up with some more breakthrough advertising. Months later the agency creatives came up with something that actually topped the lady on the tiger. It was—now hold on to your hats—a girl actually coming out of the tube. Of course you saw it—it was the breakthrough campaign of another nationally distributed competitor. And so another year and a couple more test cities went down the drain. The test in another area was completely foiled when, just as the test was about to begin, Vitalis dropped twelve-ounce samples in the area, taking most of the men in that area out of the market for a considerable time.

Between having their campaigns preempted and their test markets screwed up by competitive samples, close to ten years went by without a successful market test. By then, Union Carbide was just about up to its you-know-what with all that magic ingredient. So they called in the rest of the hair guys and offered it to all of them. And that's when the flood of men's clear gel hair groomers all hit the marketplace. Just as P&G had suspected all those years, it was a good idea. It's just too bad they blew their ten-year lead trying to prove it to themselves.

If you're wondering why they're so hooked on careful market testing before they bring out a new product, let me tell you about just one case when a little more time in the testing stage would have saved them a lot of money and trouble.

No sooner had Lever Brothers' Dove come out and grabbed a big slice of the bath and complexion market than the natives in Cincinnati became restless and wanted a similar product.

84

(In marketing, imitation is not only the sincerest form of flattery, it's a sure sign you've got a winner on your hands, and Lever Brothers did.) The P&G entry in this field, when tested in the test tube, seemed to behave just like Dove—maybe even more so. Now if there was one little problem with Dove in the consumer's opinion, it was that it tended to get a little soft and mushy in the soap dish. But all that softness evidently was just further proof of the yummy, good-for-the-skin creams that were in the bar, and so the women put up with this little drawback. Like I said, the P&G entry did all that Dove did—maybe more, including going to glop when wet.

The market had been sampled with sliver-sized samples of the product. When these little slivers went gooey in the bather's hand, she evidently felt it was because the sliver was so small and never gave it a second thought. And if she did, she certainly didn't mention it to P&G in their little evaluation questionnaire that went out with the sample.

The consumer reaction had been splendid. They loved it, they really did. Encouraged by this happy acceptance of their new product, P&G geared up big and started stocking up all the grocers' shelves. At the same time they began their advertising which had also tested well. The first week or two, there were broad grins all over the Midwest. They had another winner on their hands—they were sure. Plans were being pushed forward for a quick national introduction. No point in letting all those customers stay in Dove's pocket.

A few weeks later, the grins were replaced with furrowed brows, and a pulse-taking team was dispatched to find out why the product wasn't continuing to sell. Sales had dropped off—which was a euphemism for just about stopped. What had seemed a slight inconvenience in a sliver-sized bar turned into a major catastrophe in the full bath-size bar. No sooner did it hit the water than it went completely to a soft squishy gel in the bather's hand. In fact, it was impossible to take even a quickie shower and keep the bar in any sort of shape.

You can imagine then what happened to it if it joined you in any kind of a lolling relaxing bath. It must have been a bit like finding yourself suspended like cut-up fruit in a firming gelatin mold. All in all, not a terribly pleasant experience no matter how many wonders you felt the treatment was doing for your complexion. To make matters even worse for this badly bruised blossom in P&G's garden of new delights, once out of the offending water the bar never returned to its original shape and hardness. So there you were, left after that first shower with a gelatinous mass lying about your bathroom until you had the intestinal fortitude to scoop it up and give it a proper burial. From that unpleasant experience, we all learned that it is best to sample the full-size product. That's why, of course, sales had fallen off so perceptibly after an initial glowing report. No one in his right mind could have been persuaded to buy a second bar—and the number of people not in their right minds hardly seemed a market worth going after.

When the kink in the product is less obvious, it may not be traced back until after national introduction—and then it's the advertising that gets blamed. That was the case with Zest. It had had a fantastically successful introduction, but the sales just didn't seem to hold over the long run; there wasn't a large band of really loyal bathers developing. In fact, as time went on and sales began to drop off, it became increasingly clear to us in our ivory tower in NY that something was amiss with the product. At the same time, it was becoming increasingly obvious out in Suds City that something was wrong with the advertising. A quickie survey among people who had stopped using Zest showed that they felt it was too harsh a product. Given this piece of intelligence, the boys in Cincinnati were convinced that the claim, "For the first time in your life feel really clean," gave the product too harsh an image.

So the pressure was on to soften the product's image with a change in advertising. All those marvelous, refreshing shots of people plunging in and out of the surf were scuttled, and we started pushing Zest as a complexion bar. (Would you believe pushing a product that people thought was too harsh for bath and shower use as a complexion bar? Neither did anyone else.) But this was just the beginning of the Alice in Wonderland game. We flooded the screens with pictures of pretty young things massaging Zest lather into their complexions, but still the sales curve went down. Then we started showing babies in our commercials. You can't beat babies for softening your image. Frankly, however, a few of us diehards in the copy department felt it was a hopeless task because by then the agency's research department had gotten around to some really in-depth research. When people said they'd stopped using Zest because it was too strong, researchers snapped right back: "What makes you think it's strong?" Quick as bunnies, because your average consumer is nobody's fool, a lot of them returned the volley: "Because I broke out in this itchy rash after I'd used it for a while."

As soon as this news reached the agency, the chips were down and we all started writing in that tunnel with no escape. I mean, I'd faced creative challenges before that, but trying to cure the consumer's rash with a softer-imaged commercial was even more than I thought I could handle. Throughout it all, the boys in Cincinnati remained, at least in meetings with the agency, firmly convinced it was the advertising that was making everybody break out in a rash.

But I don't want you to think that P&G were the only ones with new product problems. It's just that some of their mistakes were a tiny bit unforgettable, and their successes are so

87

well known they hardly bear repeating. Their friendly rivals clustered on Park Avenue had more than their fair share of false starts, too. I remember working on one product that Colgate wrote off as a total loss—with one minor change it was marketed successfully by two or three other firms.

In the mid 1960's, when we were still riding the crest of a rapidly growing economy, and affluence was our most obvious characteristic, the high-domed boys in research came up with what they thought was the biggest breakthrough since sliced bread. They had managed to simulate the taste and crunch of bacon in a meatless product.

Although the formulation was a secret, I had the feeling it was made of soybean or sawdust. Great for a starving nation— but in fat cat America? Anyhow, there was much excitement about it, for reasons that now escape me completely. When word of this breakthrough reached the agency's creative department, we began racking our brains for a suitable selling idea. Even sight unseen it seemed to have a limited market at best. There were the people who liked bacon but lacked refrigeration facilities (a smallish group one would assume), people who kept a kosher home but had a craving for bacon (where would people in a kosher home *get* a craving for bacon?). Or it might also make a nice taste change for vegetarians and any religious group that was against killing. (This seemed like a rather small market, too, considering how few people really ever rally around pigs as a conservation issue.) Then there were the people who liked bacon for breakfast but didn't have time to mess around with all that broiling or frying. This seemed like the likeliest group at which to aim our advertising.

Because the product was made of various unnatural, unmentionable ingredients, it did have one big advantage over real bacon: It was completely fat free. This certainly must have some appeal for weight watchers, we figured, and their number is legion. So by combining the hurried breakfast eater with the dieter, we assumed we had a sizable market lined up. Now all we had to do was present our story in the most attractive way.

We knew from some home research (we'd asked each other) that one of the big drawbacks of cooking real bacon was getting rid of the cooked out fat. With this irrefutable piece of intelligence under my belt and a picture of our ultimate consumer in mind, I suggested we name the product Lean. It was received enthusiastically on all sides, and so the product was named.

Lean could actually be eaten as it came, in little strips in foil packaging, but we'd heard that the flavor could be improved by slipping it, foil wrapper and all, into the toaster to heat. So my headline seemed a natural: "Now, if you've time for toast, you've time for Lean." The name appealed to the weight watcher and the claim appealed to the harassed breakfast maker.

Delighted with our efforts, we took off with high hopes down Park Avenue for a taste testing session one afternoon. But before we were actually shown the product, there was the usual amount of speechmaking from the client's boys about what a challenge it had been coming up with this product. They told in loving detail all the work that had gone into its development and how pleased they were with themselves and their efforts. After such a buildup, the agency people who had skipped lunch to be properly receptive for such a product were salivating noticeably. In our minds' eye, we were expecting something just this side of a suckling pig with an apple stuck in his mouth.

Maybe that's why we were all so disappointed when the samples were brought out. Maybe, but mostly I think it was the product itself which was so disappointing. After working on the idea for several weeks, building up quite a head of steam creatively, I'm not exactly sure what I was expecting to see and taste, but it certainly wasn't what they put down in front of me that afternoon.

It lay on the plate like so many little strips of cardboard, flat in a way bacon can never be, matte finished the way only cardboard can be, and a dreary color that I suppose a piece of bacon could carry off if it were really crunchy, curly, and shiny. Masking our feelings, we began to nibble at it hesitantly. Actually, the taste wasn't bad. The little gnomes in their test tubes had captured the flavor and the crunch of bacon. What really turned you off was the look of the product. Much as we hated to eat and run, we did just that. After all, how long can you put up a brave front on an empty stomach? Back at the agency, after seeing and tasting the product, I was convinced a more appropriate name than Lean would be Facon. Like a bad dream, it just wouldn't go away. And before they consumer taste-tested it, where it died the death it so rightly deserved, the client insisted we see and taste fake turkey, fake ham, and other totally unnecessary and unnatural developments.

You can imagine my surprise when a couple of years later I found Bac-os on my grocer's shelf and fell madly in love with them. Those clever souls out in Minneapolis had gone one step beyond us. Realizing it was the eye and not the taste buds that gave it away as a fake, they just did what every homemaker does when she wants to add bacon flavor to a dish. They crumbled it up. If only one of us had thought of that, we might have prevented a real disaster.

So badly disappointed were they with this entry into the ersatz food market, that Colgate decided to try a food entry that was all food—no foolin'. It was a baked apple chip snack—about the size of a potato chip—with the same crunch but no grease and a wonderful apple-y flavor. The product really was apple slices that had been quick baked to a crunchy crispness. This time I thought they had a winner even after seeing and tasting it. We suggested they call them Snapples and could hardly wait to get this one launched.

Colgate tried it out upstate where apples come from and everyone is an apple maven. Samples were distributed and it really looked like a success. Distribution had just begun when we came a cropper: Unless the product was literally hermetically sealed, those crunchy little apple chips just drank up all the moisture in the air and reconstituted themselves back to soggy apple slices. At great expense and even greater ingenuity, a suitable package was designed for them and it worked just fine until it was opened the first time. Without the manual dexterity and patience of a diamond cutter, no one could successfully reclose the package. Certainly no little kid could. So another one went down the drain.

After you've lived through a few new product introductions, seen some fail in the lab, seen others make it to test market only, and then seen those happy few which make it through to national distribution and a certain amount of success, you become like a Jewish mother about them. You want to make sure they get the proper shelf space, adequate distribution, a good spot in the local newspaper ad or a good time slot on television. By the time a new product is successfully launched, you couldn't feel closer to it if you'd invented it. That's why it's so heartbreaking when, because of intramural politics, a new product is moved from one agency to another.

It happened to Rita Picker who had worked a year at D'Arcy on Handi Wipes. I mean, what a crazy idea if you'd never heard it before—throwaway cleaning cloths you actually went out and bought! What's wrong with old undershirts, right? That was Rita's first reaction, too, but before they went into test market she'd come up with a couple of smashing commercials that proved throwaway cleaning cloths were just what the world was waiting for.

You can imagine how she felt on the set where they were photographing her commercials when she discovered among the great gathered mass of humanity, the gentlemen from the agency that was to inherit the account the next day. How do you feel when commercials you wrote are really selling a product and another agency is taking all the glory—to say nothing of the billing? Lousy—that's how you feel.

And that's precisely how I felt when, after working on an introductory campaign for Ultra Brite for well over a year, a clash of personalities between agency and client forced the product to move out of the shop just before it went national.

Introducing a new toothpaste is like introducing a new detergent in many ways. In the first place, everyone has one, so you've got to switch them from their old-time favorite to some newcomer they don't know and couldn't care less about.

It's one thing to have a great anti-cavity story as Crest did and then follow it up with recognition by the ADA, but when you're just a Johnny-come-lately in the whitening scene, that's something else again. What we did have with Ultra Brite, as anyone who had tested the product knew, was a really great taste. An adult taste: part mint, part ether. It literally took your breath away. It was no icky-poo kid taste, that was for sure. If toothpastes were rated the way movies are, Ultra Brite would have been given an X or at least an M rating. We knew we had a live one as soon as we brushed with it. After a few days of brushing with Ultra Brite, you just couldn't go back to the dull, drab-tasting toothpaste you'd been using before.

We put together a marketing strategy that was part massive sampling and part campaign with an adult theme. We didn't come right out and use the words "sex appeal" the way the

92

succeeding agency did, we implied it. And if you know your way around sex appeal at all, you know you can get a lot further with implication and innuendo that you can with bald statements. We'd gone into test markets with our campaign and our sampling (the largest sample size ever, and a forerunner of the big samples to come). The results from the test market were really great. The market projection which we had hoped to attain was a two or three point share; what we actually got was six points. (You understand just how important each little share point is when you realize that each one represents between $3,200,000 and $3,250,000.) The product went national without any further testing, but owing to a contretemps between the head honcho at our agency and the client, it went national through another agency. Sure, it was hard to take. But even harder was switching back to my old brand of icky-poo kid's toothpaste. I didn't have much choice, did I?

After you've worked on enough new product introductions, you begin to realize that what makes a success of one and a failure of another is not always something you can control in the lab or the agency. If Wilbur had been as sophisticated as today's marketing man, his famous question back there at Kitty Hawk wouldn't have been, "Orville, will it fly?" but, "Orville, will it sell?"

CHAPTER X

"To Begin with, She's . . ."

Advertising executives (male, of course. What other sex is so eminently suited to such lofty status?) often find themselves in the same embarrassing position as the apocryphal Pope who finally got his lifetime wish to see God. When he returned to his Cardinals, who wanted to know what God really looked like, he was forced to admit, "Well, to begin with she's black."

Nine out of ten consumer products pushed by the advertising executive are aimed at females. Now bringing your flawless logic to this situation, you would assume that a female copywriter would have the inside track. Wrong. Having married and bedded a consumer of his very own, every male account executive feels he has the ultimate consumer panel right on the next pillow every night. And while conference rooms echo with remarks like "My wife thinks . . ." and "My wife says . . . ," oddly enough no one has ever heard a woman remark, "My husband thinks. . . ."

Products either outrageously overpriced or obviously unnecessary are aimed at that demographic group known affectionately to the research guys as "upper income, better educated female." For such consumers, the head-on-the-next-pillow

94

kind of research works fine. But when a product is to be mass marketed, a more objective way must be found to second-guess the reactions of females living out there beyond Darien or Beekman Place.

This is where the consumer survey, a door-to-door thing or an in-depth study of a captive group, comes in. This method is also called into use in marketing a product to an upper income, better educated consumer when the brand man's wife and the account man's wife have differing attitudes. Rather than engage in a toe-to-toe battle about who's got the more demographically correct wife, usually the client and the agency agree to split the cost of going into the street.

Going into the street is literally what they do. The research company, or the agency if they've enough warm bodies within their own department, will dispatch dedicated researchers or bored housewives to ring doorbells or stop people on the street and ask them a series of questions. In nice weather this used to be a cushy kind of assignment. You could gather up your little kit of questionnaires and your clipboard and set out for Central Park. There, in the merry sunshine, you could find countless women who were bored with the enforced chatter of two-year-olds and were more than willing to cooperate and tell all.

All kinds of research were done this way; mock-ups of ads a client was too chicken to run or that were too controversial back at the agency would be taken out and flashed at consumers to see who took offense, who misunderstood the ad, and if anybody really liked it.

You can see right away where a lot of your results were directly related to the researcher sent out. An establishment matron might well take offense at the Lord's Prayer if it were shown to her by a hippie. And no lonely senior citizen would take offense at anything shown him by some young lovely—

she may have been the only human being who had spoken to him in a week. He'd tell her he liked any ad under discussion if he thought it would prolong the conversation.

Owing to the previously mentioned fact that account executives are firmly convinced that their wives speak for Mrs. Upper America, researchers are most often called on to sample the opinions of the kind of people you're not apt to meet hacking around the Appawamis Golf Course. For this kind of research, a slightly more selective method than the stroll-through-the-park technique is used. A friend of mine who was then a research trainee at J. Walter Thompson, blue-eyed, blonde, fresh from the care of the nuns at Marymount, was dispatched on a nighttime assignment by people who should have known better to the corner outside Bamberger's in Newark. I guess it was some kind of initiation rite or trial by fire. Her father was so aghast when he heard of it, he sent her big brother to stand on the corner with her. We'll never know whether she'd have eventually made a crackerjack researcher or not because soon after that assignment, she switched to the cleaner, indoor work of a copywriter.

On rainy days, it was more often the men who went out from the agency's research department. Women who kidded themselves into thinking it was chivalry that made the men volunteer on the wet weather work didn't know some of the researchers I knew. Slipping their questionnaires under their Burberrys, they'd head for a Third Avenue bar where cheap whiskey and even cheaper advice were dispensed. There in snug camaraderie with the unemployed and the bartender, they would fill out the questionnaires at their leisure. When their creative powers lagged, they would turn to the bartender for his opinion on everything from a proposed layout to the design of a new package. For a couple of years, the bartender at

P.J.Clarke's had one of the loudest voices in the marketing decisions made by the executives at SSC&B.

In addition to the research departments inside agencies, there are also masses of organizations that do nothing at all but research. Clients often call on them when the agency's research department is not large enough to handle a project, is too busy, or is suspect. I worked on a food account which for years had used the agency's research department to test their advertising and any new ideas they were thinking of coming out with. In the twenty or twenty-five years the agency had been doing this research, they'd never got back one single negative finding. It's the kind of thing that can make a client either very sure of himself or very unsure of his agency's research. You can hardly blame the agencies, though; it's like asking a mother to criticize her child's piano recital.

Even research done by outside firms can be suspect, which is probably why the ad trade journals are now carrying stories about the research business policing its own activities. But it's a tough business to clean up when so many of its inaccuracies come more from human frailty than downright dishonesty. A top account type at one of the biggest agencies has been trying for years to sell his client on putting out a new line of cold soups. (Not the kind you keep in the freezer, but the kind you keep on the shelf and just chill to serve.) Anyhow, the idea went like gangbusters through all the meetings at the agency. The lady copywriter on the account devised and whipped up some really yummy samples, and everybody on the account who had a taste was convinced that it was a truly great idea.

But somewhere between the Park Avenue kitchen and the soup vats at the factory, the whole soufflé fell. And when the little research lady actually got out into the field taste testing the company-prepared samples, the opinions were about as negative as you can get.

97

This, of course, was a great blow to the folks back at the agency who were sure they had a real winner on their hands. Every time the account type is tempted to reopen the idea, he looks at those research findings, has second thoughts about it, and takes the research lady out to lunch. She in turn goes back to her files, reinterprets the findings, and comes up with a slightly more positive report. Listen, if he takes her to enough lunches and they rethink those research figures enough, they may be back to thinking they've got a great idea on their hands yet.

Computers and sophisticated analysis systems are making their way into research just as they are into every other simple form of life. And the days when you strolled out into the field and started buttonholing people for opinions and reactions are almost a thing of the past. Now there are learned PhDs who work in some sinister relationship with maps, computers, and formulae. Their shtick is known variously as the national probability sample or the block sampling method. Anyhow, the pros in this area are pulling down salaries in the neighborhood of fifty grand a year for this specialty. Given a map of any city, they can at great expense, without ever leaving their desks, without even so much as a glance out the window, pinpoint the addresses that should be visited to give a representative sampling or reading of opinions in any particular city.

I'm not saying it isn't scientifically sound and a big step forward and all in taking the nation's pulse, but what happens when you pinpoint doorbells this way is that once in a while you pinpoint a doorbell on an empty lot or a house of ill repute. Far be it from me to imply that ladies of the evening don't have just as much right to an opinion about a new detergent ad as their sisters of the morning, but you can bet your Neilsen share, despite the importance of clean sheets in their line of work, it'll be a cold day in July before we see one of these sequined lovelies leaning against her Whirlpool or May-tag rapping with Mrs. Ima Consumer.

Despite all the giant steps forward man and machine are making in the area of turning research into a far more scientific tool of the trade, there is still that ultimate little researcher out there on her own who can and does—unbeknownst to the client who is picking up the sizable tab for the research—throw a monkey wrench into the elaborate master plan. And though we can get a couple of men to the moon, we don't seem to have any clue about how to get these little lady researchers to the right doorbells of the right consumers.

A friend of mine, who has for some time written advertising for a big food company, had kind of an unnerving experience with one of these ladies just recently. The experience itself was not particularly unnerving, it was the implication of the incident that set my friend's teeth on edge. As a writer for a number one seller, she was used to having her work second-guessed by research and so her creative efforts were preconditioned by past research, questionnaires, and meetings with Mrs. Consumer. She knew from experience the kind of clout this research carries back in the conference rooms of the agency.

She had just arrived at her apartment after a hard day at the agency, trying to compromise creativity with hard core consumer findings, when her doorbell rang and a sweet little grey-haired motherly type announced that she was doing a survey of beer drinkers for a brewery's ad agency.

"I'm sorry but I'm not a beer drinker," my friend said, starting to close the door.

"Oh, please let me in. You're the last person I have to get today, and my feet are really killing me."

"You can come in if you'd like, but I'm afraid I'm not going to be much help with your survey."

Easing herself into the down cushions, the researcher slid off her shoes, spread her forms in front of her on the coffee table, and said, "Now don't you worry about that. You just answer a few little questions for me and I'll take care of the rest of it. How much beer do you drink a day?"

"I told you I'm not a beer drinker."

"But you must have had a glass sometime, haven't you?"

"Well, yes, but. . . ."

"That's all I want to know, dearie. There's no need to be shy about drinking beer. I do it myself, and wouldn't mind having one right now." Her eyes slid in the direction of the kitchen—all in vain. "And I just talked to a lady upstairs, right in this very building, who says she drinks two or three bottles of beer a day." (My friend knew the lady in question was actually being far too modest in her estimate.) "I'll just put you down as one bottle a day. What's your favorite brand?"

"The last beer I drank was at a barbecue this past summer, and I believe it was Löwenbrau."

"That's not on my list. I'll just write down Gablinger's—not many people have mentioned that one."

"Don't you realize that's dishonest?"

"If you'd spent the whole day tramping the city trying to find women who admit they drink beer, you might not be so honest yourself," the research maven returned huffily, pulling her papers together. "I'll just fill in the rest of this when I get home."

By now my friend was really incensed. "I realize you're probably tired, but so am I. I'm tired of having research that's probably no more reliable than what you're doing right now forced down my throat as gospel. Don't you realize some beer copywriter may lose a whole campaign—or even his job—as a result of this survey you're doing?"

And just before the door closed behind her, she turned

and replied, "That's the worst thing you can think of to happen?"

My friend, who has a philosophical bent, sat down with her Scotch on the rocks and started to think of a lot worse things that could happen—especially to little lady researchers.

Despite its foibles, research is the only thing a writer has going for her when she sits down at that blank page.

When we were about to introduce flavored, dissolvable Knox Gelatine Drink, research told us a lot about the women who were our target audience: the great majority of women were aware that Gelatine was good for their nails, and in fact a high percentage of them had actually tried Knox but just found it too unpleasant to go on with for the full 90 days required. Knowing this helped me tremendously. In double page spreads we announced: "Now for every woman who knows she should . . . but wouldn't or couldn't take gelatine for her nails KNOX ANNOUNCES THE FIRST GELATINE THAT DISSOLVES COMPLETELY, BUT COMPLETELY." Nothing tricky, nothing funny, nothing you come away from the page humming. But it not only sold out Knox's supply of the new product and kept the plant running nights, it also was, on a dollar per dollar basis, the most successful introductory campaign that year. So successful was it that when a few months after it broke, another agency went to Johnstown to pitch the account, the client asked them only one thing: how could they top an introduction like that? "We'd have bought single pages instead of spreads," the agency said. The answer showed they could think on their feet, but they didn't get the account.

Because agencies and clients have gotten wind of the way a lot of research is actually done, or maybe just because they refuse to believe some of the results they've been handed in the past, another kind of consumer research has come along. In this, the consumer is brought to the researcher and other agency personnel. It's called in-depth research and it is usually done in groups with a psychologist or psychiatrist asking the questions, while the executives and creative types from the agency and the client watch and listen.

This is an expensive kind of research, so it is hardly ever done just to get opinions on headlines, although it is sometimes used for that if all other forms of arm twisting on the part of the agency have failed to get a campaign OKd. Mostly though, it is used to probe into how people really feel about certain products and companies, and how they cotton to the idea of a new product the client may be planning to bring out.

These little seminars, as you can imagine, sometimes open up more cans of worms than are wise. What the leader has to do, of course, is keep everybody talking freely, but hopefully with a civil tongue in her head. Once emotions are aroused and hostility is expressed or even implied, the research goes down the drain because the irate ladies will say things in the heat of these encounters they wouldn't dream of in the cool calm of a written questionnaire. When the moderator is good, you can get down to the nitty-gritty really quickly—maybe too quickly. At least you're usually kept beyond the firing range.

In order to keep the consumer panel as relaxed and open as possible, the team from the agency and the client usually retires to an adjoining room, listening to the proceedings over an intercom system, and watching through a one-way mirror.

When Vicks was about to launch a new antacid a while back, I found myself over at the Plaza attending more of these one-way mirror sessions than I felt was good for my digestive system. After you hear enough of these tortured people tell the nice moderator what makes their digestive tracks clutch up, all you want to do is drop your pencil and pad, run to the next room, pat their hands, and say, "There, there, everything will be all right." It's a funny thing about people with digestive trouble, 90 per cent of what's wrong in their gut seems to be directly traceable to what's wrong in their head.

Most of the people who were interviewed in that particular series of be-ins were middle-aged and older women who'd seen more of life than they really should have. But one day, as the group from the client and the agency were huddled there in the dark behind the one-way mirror, a young man, blond wavy hair curling sensitively down over his Bill Blass collar, walked into the discussion room. He spotted the big, baroquely framed mirror behind which we were all quietly huddled, rushed up to it, and inches away from us began lovingly to rearrange his languorous locks. It was a tense moment for the group. First guy to flinch was it, right? As the only girl in the room I thought it might help if I giggled. It helped enough so that I'm still wondering whether it was the account man or the brand man who was doing all the heavy breathing. You're at these sessions to learn—so you learn.

If you had your druthers about the one-way mirror sessions you'd pick to attend, probably top of the can miss list would be a DuPont one, agreed? Maybe, but you'd have missed one of the greatest girly shows since La Guardia cooled the action.

As the kingpin in nylon, DuPont has to have one of the biggest interests going in pantyhose. So a bunch of lovelies were invited to drop by their friendly local Madison Avenue shop one afternoon and bare their souls about what they liked and didn't like about the nylon pantyhose that were then on the market. Big afternoon of yawns, right? Wrong. When a lovely starts rapping about what's wrong with pantyhose, words just don't seem to suffice. So there they all were, on the other side of that one-way mirror, just inches away from the eyeballs of some of the biggest fiber guns in the country, lifting their skirts and pointing out where the welt went astray and what was wrong with the crotch. There are guys in Delaware today who still talk about that little piece of research.

103

CHAPTER XI

Across the Hudson and Into the Woods
(The Dyspeptic Encounter)

Despite my mother's warnings, there I was, headed through the dark December night toward a New Jersey hotel with a married man at my side. But it was digestive disorders, not sexual appetites that had brought us together. At a time when all right-thinking young women were dividing their time between last minute Christmas drinking and shopping, I was slated for five fun-filled days and nights in the Jersey woods, with an ill-assorted crowd of research and brand men from the agency and the client. Bob Cratchit's brood would have been hard put to force a smile under the circumstances.

The agency had been working for several months on exploratory campaigns for a new antacid the client was hoping to launch soon. Under the heading of "exploratory campaigns" goes all the preliminary creative work that clients feel is so necessary. It's called exploratory only because it all must be done in a dark vacuum where facts about the product are either not available or non-existent because the product itself is still just a vague dream in the back of some scientific type's head. The product we were about to launch was supposed to do everything all the other products in the field did, but quicker, better, and with about half the dosage.

This may not seem like such a big deal to you if your self-medication has been limited to popping pills or capsules into your mouth, but if you've ever been a stomach person (as opposed to a back or head person), you've undoubtedly dealt with those thick viscous liquids that you have to take by the tablespoonful. And not just one tablespoon, either—two, sometimes three. I mean you really have to feel rotten to cope with these cures. So we felt we were on to a good thing. Especially the account executive who was a stomach person, having graduated from the ulcer course and gone on to all kinds of wonderful, exotic complications and secondary symptoms. He was typecast for the account.

Besides being able to pack all the relief your stomach can use into such a tiny dose, the product was scheduled as a more effective stomach liner than anything then on the market. That's why I wanted the introductory advertising to announce that we were "launching the littlest liner" and show our little bottle inside one of those big ugly bottles the competition came in—like a ship's model. I made the suggestion early on, long before I came to realize just how seriously stomach people take their troubles.

I was really more interested in this product and its consumers than I had any right to be, because I had always thought of myself as a potential stomach person. Having swallowed whole all the widely spread tales of advertising being an ulcer-making kind of business, I felt an ulcer was probably a status symbol. I was afraid my inability to grow an ulcer of my own was probably standing between me and a vice presidency. So not too far down on my list of things to do some day was: develop an ulcer. But like all card-carrying hypochondriacs, I wanted to make sure there was a quick cure for anything I intended to talk myself into. To tell the truth, having been in on this product and its attendant research, I've decided never to have one, despite its status.

The purpose of this December romp in Jersey was twofold: It was to combine the biggest and deepest in-depth interviews with a kind of commercialized marathon encounter group. We big city types were not only out there in the Jersey hills trying to get to know the suffering consumer, but we were also supposed to get to know each other better. It was felt by the client's management that the better you knew your agency, the better they would work for you. Can't prove it by me; shortly after this séance, the client took his still unproduced product to another agency. It was also slated to be the granddaddy of all brainstorming sessions. Without any phones or the presence of loved ones to interrupt or distract us, we were supposed to be capable of feats of creativity unknown under other circumstances.

While I can hardly say the week was an unmitigated success, I can't say that *none* of the goals was achieved. God knows, I learned more about heartburn, acid indigestion, ulcers, and spastic stomachs than a girl has any need to know.

It was an ill-fated week right from the start. The first car we rented had no brakes and had to be returned before we got more than a block from the rental office. Returning a car with no brakes is not the easiest thing in the world. The second car was a big improvement and the drive through the Jersey night went smoothly.

The festivities were planned for a hotel in Morristown, a small town that prides itself on its pre-revolutionary heritage and the fact that so little has changed since then. A charming residential community, their shtick is that they have avoided all the problems of urban sprawl and have remained pure and unsullied by commercialism and overcrowding. There is no road—in a state fairly honeycombed with big reds and big

106

blues on the map—that goes directly to Morristown. Washington spent two winters there, probably because he couldn't find his way out. And Lafayette is supposed to have visited him while he was there. How he ever made his way from France to Morristown is beyond me. Finding the place from New York was practically impossible. But many cold hours after leaving New York, having been through every bedroom community on that side of the Hudson, we finally did manage to locate Morristown and the hotel. It is a great sprawling affair built in the psuedo early American style that seems torn between Williamsburg and Sturbridge. What a hotel of that immense size is doing in a place like Morristown, I'd rather not know.

Needless to say, by the time we arrived, the rest of the troops had already been through the cocktail hour as well as dinner, and we were offered a few dry sandwiches. But the quality of the food mattered little since before we could get to it, the first of the uptight pre- and post-ulcerous types began arriving, and it hardly seemed fair under the circumstances to be wolfing down food in front of them.

Best I explain the physical setup of the room we were literally to live in for the next five days. It was a long, narrow, low-ceilinged room with windows only along one side, making ventilation a physical impossibility. A U-shaped table that would comfortably (now there's a euphemism) seat at least twenty filled most of the room. At the far end, opposite the only door, was an amazing array of electronic equipment, for every golden word of the proceedings was to be recorded for posterity. At various times during the ordeal, a lackey from the hotel's room service department would wheel in a little cart with corrosive coffee and Danish or sandwiches, depending on the time of day.

The first group of stomach people brought in that night were listed on the program as "Adult males, mint users." Such a category, of course, allows the research firm that lined up our victims considerable leeway. And after seeing and hearing their harvest of humanity that night, I must say they availed themselves of every bit of the leeway at their disposal.

When that first session broke up—far into the night—the top man on the client's team invited us all to his suite for nightcaps. It seemed like the best idea I'd heard all day. I grasped at a Scotch on the rocks, took a deep swallow, and instead of the usual warming glow that follows, felt the hot sear of heartburn race down my esophagus. My digestive system was already replaying the symptoms my mind had been grappling with earlier that evening. I realized then that for someone as suggestible as I am, it was going to be a rotten five days. I was so right.

We usually interviewed men at night and women during the day for the obvious reason that any man supporting a pre-ulcerous condition was more than likely to be gainfully employed during the day. Not only were the interviewees divided up by sex and, to a degree, by age, but they were also divided up by the seriousness of their stomach problems. Really the most engaging group were the ones who had such minor complaints as heartburn after an evening of bowling, beer, pepperoni pizza, more beer, raw onions, and maybe a few tacos washed down by even more beer. When their stomachs sent up distress signals as a result of all this, they'd pop a little antacid mint in their mouths and be right back at it. Obviously, there was nothing wrong with this group that a portable stomach pump wouldn't have cured. They were not the market we were after.

Our potential consumer had more serious complaints—and boy, did they ever complain! Reading ahead on the program for the five days, one could see these coming: "Adult males (or females) who regularly take an antacid more than once a day." As the week drew on, we found ourselves dealing with progressively heavier and heavier dosers, as they were affectionately known among us ad types. The complaints ranged from minor frustrations with housework and children to one woman's conviction that her mother-in-law was trying to poison her. She was always sick after eating at her in-laws'. The light dosers, the ones who relied on little mints for relief, usually felt the distress symptoms directly after eating some forbidden spice. But the serious sufferers, the big dosers, often had "attacks" that seemed in no way connected with eating. They'd often wake up in the middle of the night in such pain that they were sure they were having a heart attack. Or they would feel the symptoms coming on on the way to work or on the way to school. You didn't have to be a psychologist to see what was really eating these people.

The more serious their emotional and psychological hang-ups were, the heavier dosers they were. These were the consumers we were after with our product, the ones who were used to taking large doses of those chalky, clinging liquids. That's why, to this day, I think the product should have been positioned as the antacid for when "its not something you ate, but something that's eating you."

One thing that week in the woods did for me, it cured me of the snobbish notion that an ulcer is the status disease of the seventies. There are people out there who have never seen the inside of a board room, who are being eaten alive by frustrations, neuroses, and tensions. And the fact that you—sitting across the green baize table from them—can see their problem in everything they say and do, isn't one iota of help to them. If you think your mother always favored your older sister—the one she's always slipping the family treasures to, the one with the goody-goody kids and the husband who manages the supermarket—all the talk in the world isn't going to keep your

109

stomach from turning on you every time you see that sister or hear your mother rave about her.

The most unforgettable sufferer we had was a young man in his mid-twenties (not the usual age for the pre-ulcerous, by the way) who worked in a garage owned by his father. Of all the things there are to be in the world, the last thing he wanted to be was a garage mechanic. But it was his father's garage, his father's decision, and the ulcer this young man was growing could just as surely be credited to his father.

The days were broken up between question and answer sessions with the sufferers and talk and think sessions with just the agency and client people roundtabling it. This is when everyone got into the act of writing—and not just pithy thoughts about our product and our market. Men from the labs and R&D areas who had never seen the inside of an agency suddenly blossomed into copywriters. If you think everyone you meet at a cocktail party can write your ads better than you can, you should try locking yourself up in a room with two dozen men who have brought a product into being from a test tube. They know what they want to say about it, they just don't know how to put it into words. This last admission some of them will make shyly, while others feel the language of the lab is just right for radio, TV, and billboards. It's hard to say which is more trying, listening to the woes of the antacid takers or listening to the copy attempts of the antacid makers. It was, if you'll pardon the expression, a toss-up.

As we all sat there, hour after hour, day after day—with sessions running from early in the morning until nearly midnight—listening to the litany of suffering, a funny thing began to take place within our group. As the picture of the heavy doser as a neurotic began shaping itself in everybody's head, the account man, who had until then been an admitted heavy doser himself, felt himself more and more on the defensive. He found it harder and harder to talk about his attitude toward the competitive products as well as our own. The client, who had never admitted to needing an antacid *ever,* became more and more vocal in his denials. The week's togetherness, instead of drawing us all closer together in understanding, was really dividing us. The split was between those who had earlier admitted to having been heavy users of antacids and those who hadn't. It was like the showdown at Ulcer Gulch. First guy to burp was out.

During the first two sessions, there had been two women present from the research department of the agency. But they took to their dog sleds the second day and mushed back to New York and I was left there, the only woman in this enforced camaraderie. If the air in the room had been breathe-able, and the topic under discussion more bearable, the company might have seemed a lot more affable. As it was, I'd have been a lot happier as well as a lot more comfortable in the pre-Christmas rush in Macy's basement. That's how bad it was.

Then, on the last day of the encounters, an attractive young girl from the client's research department came to the early morning session. Must have traveled half the night, or had a hard time finding the place, I surmised from the glazed look in her eyes. I doubted if she'd had any idea of what a dreary time she'd gotten herself into. I found out I'd been wrong on all counts when I talked to her during the coffee break. As a researcher, she was an old hand at these encounter groups, and she had zeroed in on our New Jersey hideaway with the natural instinct of a homing pigeon.

"It's not going to be the pleasantest kind of discussion," I tried to warn her.

"Don't worry about me," she said, draining her cup of the

acrid coffee, "I've just come from three days in another part of the forest, in-depthing feminine hygiene products. This session at least has got me out of the crotch and into the digestive tract. That has to be an improvement."

CHAPTER XII

People in Palm Beach Have Bad Breath, Too

New Yorkers like to kid themselves into thinking they're always first with the most, the pace setters, the foretasters of things to come. Actually when it comes to new products, New Yorkers, like betrayed husbands, are usually the last to know. New York City just doesn't happen to be a good test market. It's too big, too expensive, too diverse—and there are too many complicating factors in this market. So by the time any new product appears on the shelves in Manhattan, it's really old hat in some culturally advanced spot like Wichita or Akron.

This rule of thumb applies only to products that eventually become nationally distributed. With its size and its marvelous ethnic mix, of course, New York City is a perfect market—forget test—if you're planning to bring out a new nosh or a new knish. Maybe you don't have to be Jewish to love Levy's, but you'd be crazy to try to launch such a loaf in Salt Lake City.

If New York is too big, too expensive, and too hard to read to be a good test market for most products, what does make a good test market? A lot of technical things go into the choice, of course. The city has to have a reasonably typical ethnic mix, a suitable choice of media available, and hopefully not be

113

the same city a competitor is using for his test. On top of these logical considerations, throw in the emotional ones. The final decision about which city to use as a test market is also influenced by such immeasurables as its proximity to a big resort, its climate, or its reputation as a fun spot. That explains the now classic statement from a brand man about to market a new mouthwash. Plugging for a test area where he'd really enjoy doing the store checks, he announced to assembled marketing mavens, "People in Palm Beach have bad breath, too." Transparent as it was, it was a hard argument to refute.

Before any of you New Yorkers out there start getting sulky or petulant about not being in on the ground floor, count your blessings. The products that hit the test markets, for reasons almost too deep for such a work as this, are often far from the happy combination of characteristics that finally winds up in the product when it goes national. There's really no way of knowing whether or not you live in a test market until you live through the introduction of a product that still had more than its fair share of kinks yet to be worked out when it went into distribution in your home town.

Even before a product gets as far as its first test market, millions of dollars and man-hours have often gone into its development. So you really can't blame the manufacturer for rushing it out while it still has a few hangups: He wants to see a little of his investment money coming home to roost. And in the case of a really new product, there's always the chance that if you don't hurry, your competitor can beat you into the market place.

Picking test markets can be tricky. And if you overlook just one little thing about a market, you can wildly misread your results. It happened once in Chicago. A scarcity of the necessary materials for making toothpaste tubes during the war years had forced this latest development, a liquid toothpaste, from the R&D people. It came a little late, of course, but once you've put that kind of money into development, the fact that the war has come to a hasty end can't stop you from marketing it. So it was brought out and test marketed in Chicago. At that time the Windy City was literally the crossroads of the country with its rail lines and wholesalers spreading out in all directions. The sell-in was an enormous success. No one bothered to figure out that all that liquid toothpaste wasn't going onto Chicago teeth, but was being shuttled off in all directions. Therefore it appeared to be a lot better seller than it actually was. Which, as it turned out, was a good thing.

Owing to the misreading of the Chicago results, the manufacturer was sure they had a big winner and went rushing pell-mell into national distribution. Now there was a kind of odd thing about the formulation of that liquid toothpaste: When in the course of human events, the toothliquid came in contact with a person who had a certain calcium level and happened to live, by chance, in an area with a certain mineral content in the tap water, it turned their teeth black. All the king's horses and all the king's men couldn't put white teeth back in those unfortunate mouths. Fortunately, or unfortunately, depending on your calcium level, this combination was such a rarity that it was literally years before the ADA was ever able to trace this rash of black teeth to its source. By then, people had tired of watching the toothliquid run through the bristles of their toothbrushes and down the drain, and the product had been withdrawn.

Let's face it, a formulation goof like that would be hard to pick up in the labs or even in a test market. But some product mistakes should really be picked up long before the first test market. Like the first liquid shortening that I ever worked on. It was supposed to be a first in more ways than one—and it certainly was.

If you've ever messed around with the scooping, scraping, and general mucking around you have to do to get the proper measurement of a solid shortening, you can see right away why this product would be welcomed with open arms by the little homemakers of the world, especially the bakers. The product seemed to have everything going for it. It even poured out a nice buttery yellow (in fact it looked and smelled a lot like melted butter). When I was called in to give it resuscitation, it had been languishing in test markets for years, and they were close to running out of cities to introduce it in. Actually it was still in test market somewhere when I eventually picked up my pencils and pushed on to another agency.

If you bake at all, you can see right away that there would be no challenge at all to come up with a really zingy demonstration of the product's superiority. Without stretching your imagination a bit, I'm sure you can see the miles of film that must have been shot showing how much easier and quicker it was to bake with our liquid shortening; little fixed races like you used to run in high school algebra. Housewife A had our liquid shortening, and she was pitted against poor pitiful Housewife B who still had hard-to-measure, hard-to-cut, solid shortening. The results of these little races were as much in doubt as the winner in a race of drugged greyhounds.

For a demonstration on frying, we were a little more hard-pressed, but with a lot of fooling around with frying temperatures and spatter plus the old polyunsaturate saw, we came up with a fairly convincing show in that area as well.

Sitting on the set watching our product perform like a real trooper, I found it hard to believe that it hadn't been catapulted into national distribution years ago. In fact, the thing looked like such a sure thing I just had to know if there was something about the product the home economist who was preparing all the food for the commercial knew that I didn't know: I am not one of those writers of the new school who feels you have to live with your product to sell it. Early on, I became so disenchanted with several products I'd been assigned to that I found it difficult if not impossible to write glowingly or convincingly on the subject. As a result, I'd written on Betty Crocker Cake Mixes for years—written them into first place in fact, without ever having baked one of their cakes. Shortly after leaving BBDO, I did bake a Betty Crocker cake and was pleased as punch with the results. Should have been baking them all along, but you never know and I didn't want to take any chances and dull my girlish enthusiasm.

"How come our liquid shortening isn't the biggest fat in the fire?" I asked the motherly type hanging over the hot fat vats.

She gave me a long, hard look, and evidently the question in my baby blues passed muster. "You really don't know, do you? I thought you were kidding." Pulling herself up to her full height which was considerable, she said, "Any cook worth her salt never uses a shortening just once for frying. She always pours it back in the can and keeps reusing it." Then with a gesture I found a bit flamboyant under the circumstances, she picked up the offending can and indicated the small pouring spout on top. "In the first place, it takes the patience of a saint to pour anything back into that spout. And in the case of this particular shortening, once you pour back the shortening that's been heated, it solidifies just like bad old brand X, forming a solid layer on top. All the rest of the liquid shortening underneath is permanently sealed in the can, making it handy to use as a doorstop but not really much help in baking or frying."

I rushed to the account executive, who was hovering over the model in a far corner of the set, with this damning piece of intelligence. He seemed oddly more upset about losing the model's attention than he did about the inevitable loss of the next test market.

"Sure, sure," he said. "They know about that little problem and their R&D guys are working on it. Have been for years as a matter of fact."

"Then why don't we stop advertising it until they get it fixed. We're using up all our campaigns and test markets."

"No, no, honey." He spoke like an MD talking to a mental defective. "Can't do that or the client will think we don't have faith in the product. And that would look bad. Would never do."

That was the most interesting day I ever spent on a set. I learned a very important rule about test marketing for a big company. The pressure is always on to get a new product into test market and, hopefully, into national distribution. The client is anxious to see some return or at least some encouragement for all the time and money he's spent developing the product, and of course the agency is always anxious to get some advertising into production so that they can bill the client. A mind-boggling amount of creative and research work is done by agencies for which they cannot bill the client until the product is actually being marketed and advertised. That's why you so often find a product in test market long before it should have left the lab.

The thing that makes this system hard to live with—at least from the writer's point of view—is that throughout the months it takes to work the major kinks out of the product, one good campaign after another goes down the drain. For while their research boys are fiddling with the product, their marketing men are demanding new and different campaigns. It's a rare case indeed when the perfect product and the perfect campaign hit the street at the same time. Which is just one more

118

reason why you see some of the advertising you do see and why you'll never see some much better advertising that went down the drain in Dubuque, unsung and unrecognized except by the advertising connoisseur in that test market.

At Benton and Bowles I worked for a marvelously self-contained woman, a real pro and a real lady. She was one of the most levelheaded people I was ever to meet in the business and she once gave me some good advice when I was complaining about the amount of good advertising that gets scuttled. "A good ad is one that runs." It was as simple as that. No crying over spilt campaigns, lost layouts, or beautiful bon mots. With a philosophy like that you can see how and why she has outlasted every purge and come through even the youthquake unscathed. After years of working on the introductions of new Procter & Gamble products, she never collected many awards but she has an enormously loyal following out in Suds City where sales are the ultimate measure of achievement.

Because I happen to live in Manhattan, as a consumer I don't expect to find myself dealing with new products that haven't been worked out properly. So you can imagine my surprise recently when I found myself outwitted by a brand new push-button rug shampoo. The first can I bought had a tiny little nozzle that broke off immediately in my hand, and $2.00 went out in the trash. (How do you dispose of a full pressurized can in an apartment where every incinerator carries such frightening warnings about just such things?)

At the time I thought nothing could be more frustrating than having a huge untapped can of magic suds in your hand with no way to get it onto the rug. That's what I thought until I bought the second can. (You can see what a persistent little consumer I am, once turned on by an ad or a commercial.) As soon as I lifted the cap on the second can, I allowed myself a tiny smug smile of self-satisfaction: The top had been rede-

119

signed entirely. "Must have realized their problem and straightened it out," I thought, as I upended the can over my rug and pressed the newly-designed valve. Sure enough, out came the magic foam. When I'd covered the prescribed three square feet, I released the big red button and righted the can. But still the white foam oozed out. Jiggling, tapping, and wiggling the top had no effect on the steady flow of foam. I was beginning to look like some ill-starred heroine of a bad fairy tale, standing in my carpeted kitchen with the foam building up around me like a persistent snowstorm.

Thinking quickly on my foam-covered feet, I rushed the discharging can into the bathroom and let it exhaust itself in the tub. If you think it's frustrating having a pressurized can of ingredients you can't get to, try having a pressurized can of ingredients you can't get away from. It's absolute magic the amount of foam those clever souls managed to pack into that can. I was tempted to fill up plastic bags with it and return it to Racine for repackaging, but cooler head prevailed, and I just pulled the plug on it all.

As I stood staring at that tubful of foam, I thought back to the test marketing days when I'd worked on Pledge. For the non-homemakers in the crowd, it was the first spritz-on furniture wax. Women knew that waxing was good for furniture and all of them took a special pride in their homes right after they'd waxed. But they usually only waxed their furniture once a month or even less frequently. All we had to do was to convince them that they could have all the benefits of this once-a-month job every time they dusted with Pledge, and without the usual effort. "Waxed beauty instantly as you dust" was the line I came up with, and it does my heart good to see it all these years later, still on every can of Pledge.

The kinks had been worked out of the advertising for Pledge before they had worked out the kinks in the product. But they wanted to be first out with such an item and so the one they went into test markets with was not exactly the one we all know and love today. It had an annoying little habit of building up on your furniture and became—I believe the word is—tacky. Theoretically, if a woman dusted her coffee table every day with this test market product, sometime before eternity struck there was always the possibility that the wax build-up on the coffee table would reach eye level. Fortunately, things never reached this point, but there was this tiny tacky problem. Things had a decided tendency to stick to tables that had been gone over with the first experimental batches. If you ever find yourself leafing through a 1959 issue of a magazine you can't lift from the table, you'll know you're in test market territory.

If you ever feel you've missed some of the fun and excitement of living in a test market, think about the unfortunates who got caught in the cross fire of a salad dressing-mayonnaise war. They were the test market for a product we'll call Spinblend, a real bomb if there ever was one.

For years Hellman's had enjoyed about three-quarters of the mayonnaise market and Kraft had been equally happy with about three-quarters of the salad dressing market. To shake up this happy balance, Spinblend was introduced. Unfortunately, the temperature gauge on one of the processing machines for the test market batch of the stuff had a slight sinking spell unbeknownst to the manufacturer. As a result, funny little things began forming inside the jars standing so neatly on the grocers' shelves. They weren't funny little things that could poison you, but they did form a highly volatile gas inside the jar, and whenever one of the jars was shaken or jarred the cap would fly off and salad dressing would cover everyone within shooting range. You don't have to spread yourself over too many kiddies in shopping carts, or mommies on

121

their weekly shopping tours, to make for a lot of hard feelings. So that's why Hellman's still has three-quarters of the mayonnaise market, Kraft has three-quarters of the salad dressing market, and you're very unlikely to get covered with salad dressing the next time you're in your supermarket.

CHAPTER XIII

If a Man Asks, Hang up

The women's lib groups are trying to get sexism out of them; the Bible Belt is trying to get sex out of them; the NAACP is trying to get blacks into them; copywriters are trying to get awards out of them; the TV viewer is trying to get away from them. And a little old lady out in Kansas City is having the final say about them. *Them,* of course, are the ubiquitous commercials that people outside the business find almost as irritating as people *in* the business do. It's absolutely amazing the number of people who consider themselves the ultimate experts in advertising.

I suppose the reason that every American old enough to climb out of his playpen feels like such an expert on advertising is that he's seen so much of it. One can hardly blame the viewing public for developing this jaundiced eye. Assuming you saw (have they ever decided whether it's 350 or 1,500 advertising impressions the average person receives in one day?) as many appendectomies a day as you see ads, you'd probably feel quite free to make suggestions about suturing and so forth the next time you were eyeball to eyeball with a surgeon. As a matter of fact, my doctor tells me that ever since the recent wave of materia medica on the tube, he's finding himself toe to

123

toe with more and more of his patients on his diagnoses. He told me this recently when I was trying unsuccessfully to convince him that I had something new and exotic Dr. Welby had just stumbled on that week.

But whether it's contempt born of too much familiarity or just plain inborn, one thing's for sure: With one or two possible exceptions, nobody likes the commercials that are on the air. The fact that some of the most disliked ones are pitching some of the most popular products in the marketplace says more about the caliber of the viewing and buying public than it does about those little stalwarts who actually write and produce the ads. All things considered, I think we're getting the commercials we deserve. But that's not saying we still can't do something about them.

A couple of years ago, Warwick & Legler made an interesting survey of some ten thousand homes and reported the results in *The New York Times*. This survey happens to prove what every copywriter deep down in her heart of heart knows. (Whether she'll admit it to even her psychiatrist, that's something else.) There's just no correlation between enjoying the commercial and buying the product. Among the ten most irritating commercials were those for Crest (number one in its field), Right Guard (also number one) Scope (in the top three), Secret, Ultra Brite, and Ajax (each in the top five or better in its field). Without a checklist, just listing them from memory, the most popular commercials were the following: Alka Seltzer, Ban, Benson & Hedges, Clark Gum, Hamm and Schlitz beers, Pepsi-Cola, Bayer Aspirin, Volkswagen, and Dodge. Funny thing about Dodge, they may not sell the most cars in the world, but they do seem to run the most controversial advertising. The Dodge Rebellion campaign that ran for two years and landed them on both the most liked and the most irritating lists, was followed by the Red Neck sheriff campaign that got them bounced off stations in the deep South. And P&G, who made the two negative lists (disliked and un-informative) most often, is still top dog in sales. You go figure.

The problem for the copywriter seems to come when he sits down at the typewriter, a blank yellow page in front of him and a whole lifetime of wanting to be loved and admired behind him. Especially in the late sixties, the problem was whether to write a commercial or ad that would attract the admiration and attention of your peers or one that would motivate a large number of consumers to get out there and buy your client's product. The sixties became the decade of the collectors. The writers were collecting awards, publicity, and some of the biggest money in the history of a big money business. It was a time when the economy was fat cat enough to support this kind of unrestrained, self-conscious pandering to one's ego; it was a time of the inside gag, the elbow in the rib kind of advertising. All the ethnic groups in the advertising community loved it. The average consumer, not as ethnically secure as his brothers in Adland, were not quite as happy with this turn of events as were the awards committees.

Doyle Dane Bernbach's Rheingold campaign has to stand as the classic ethnic campaign that backfired. It turned out to be far more divisive than persuasive. (One wonders sometimes how much our Vice President's style was honed in those years.) You must remember the campaign. It had a great payoff line after explaining that more Jews, more Italians, more Irish, in fact in New York, more people drank Rheingold than any other beer. They modestly admitted, "We must be doing something right." Maybe they were, but it wasn't their advertising that was right. Every time they showed one ethnic group quaffing Rheingold, they turned off every other one. You couldn't, if you tried, pick a worse group than beer drinkers to aim an ethnically divisive campaign at. The people in this country who drink beer in any considerable amounts are the same hard hats who are proving such a thorn in the side of the present liberal front. A very small percentage of the population drinks a very large percentage of the beer in this country. And because they do—and are who they are—the Schaefer campaign is right on and the Rheingold one was about as far off the target as you can get. It was another award winning, account losing campaign.

But let's get back to the copywriter face to face with his blank yellow paper. Suppose you were in his place—wouldn't you rather write a commercial that brought giggles and admiration from your peers than some drab old demonstration, name-claim thing or some trite slice of life commercial that would never make it past the jury of selection at the commercials festival? The problem as far as the advertiser was concerned was that most of the people writing commercials in the sixties would really have been a lot happier following in Neil Simon's or Dick Cavett's shoes. They were more than willing to take the big money the agencies were offering them, but they just didn't want to play by the rules; they brought their own rules to the game, *and* they brought their own judges.

Writers sat down at their typewriters each morning with at least the unconscious goal of getting laughs rather than sales. It was a great season for unemployed comics. But it turns out back at the checkout counter and the cash register, you could get a lot of laughs without getting much in the way of sales. Listen, if Alka Seltzer could have gotten as many sales as they got laughs out of Alice Playten's marshmallowed meatballs, they'd probably still be at DDB. When that sizable piece of business changed hands last winter, there was a lot of talk around Wells, Rich, Greene that what Alka Seltzer needed was hard sell in today's climate. What they actually needed was not so much hard sell as properly directed straight sell, aimed at the market they were after—not the awards juries who probably never have heartburn. And if you miss those marvelously wry delineations of just what constitutes an Excedrin headache, consider this: Excedrin sales shot up 25 per cent when they switched to the David Jansen, stand-up, hard sell spots.

The years of the collectors now seem to be over what with two of the big award collectors, Y&R and DDB, putting a tight lid on the number of festivals and contests they'll enter; and with the economy putting the squeeze on the advertiser, he now wants results not blue ribbons. Even the biggest spenders can no longer afford the care and feeding of these super-inflated creative egos. They're judging advertising by the old-fashioned criterion: How well does it sell? They're asking not who's laughing but who's buying.

What has always amazed me is the number of companies and agencies who will pay really big dollars to grab the creative efforts of some hot shot copywriter, pay even bigger dollars for the men who will supervise and edit his words, and then on top of that spend even more money second-guessing his work at the client level before putting it on the air. Once aired, they make what they consider the ultimate check. That's where the little lady in Kansas City starts to loom really large. She and a handful of her peers are phoned late in the evening after the commercial has had its first airing. Sometimes, too, they're not phoned until the next day. At that time, they will be asked to recall the commercial—play back as many points as they remember and, of course, correctly identify the product. On the strength of their responses, whole campaigns that may have taken months to develop and get OKd can go down the drain. It is also when the go ahead is given on some of the advertising you all seem to feel is so offensive to your intelligence. If, through the use of some device or slogan which you may not cotton to, the advertiser has made himself unforgettable to that little lady in Kansas City, you're stuck with that commercial at least until the agency can come up with another device or slogan that's more memorable and probably more irritating to you.

Copywriters discuss their "scores" (the percentage of little ladies who remember seeing the commercial when exposed to it) the way ball players talk up their batting averages. A high scoring commercial, like the Piels Brothers one for instance, can sometimes lead an advertiser down the primrose path to disaster. Remembering a commercial is one thing, going out and buying the product that paid for the commercial is something else again, as Warwick & Legler proved. Until some researcher comes along with a really foolproof way to measure not just attitudinal changes (which some feel they can do now) but also that hard-to-pin-down urge to buy, the advertiser and the public are going to have to muddle through with advertising that's hard to forget. The fallacy in this reasoning is obvious: Some of the advertising I find most unforgettable is for products I wouldn't give shelf room to, having tried them just once.

But whether or not you agree that memorability is the sign of a commercial's worth, that's the measuring stick that's being used, and to lick 'em you're going to have to join 'em. That's why I've developed a few suggestions—not as a copywriter but as someone who is just as upset as the next person about some of the pap that is being offered for our viewing and persuasion. A few simple rules and who knows, if we all stick to them, we may get the kind of advertising we want—rather than something a few ladies in the Midwest decree.

Which takes us back to the little lady in Kansas City. Let's assume she's made it past the formica coffee table and the plastic palm and answered her phone. After the initial preliminary exchange in which the dedicated researcher convinces Mrs. KC that he is not one of those obscene callers she's just read about in an AT&T ad, the Dedicated Researcher and Mrs. KC are off something like this:

DR: "Have you seen any television this evening?" (She can't say no, he can hear it in the background.)

Mrs. KC: "Yes, as a matter of fact, I have."

DR: "Good, did you by any chance see *To Rome with Love?*"

Mrs. KC: "Oh, yes, I never miss it. Don't you think those little girls are just the darlingest things you've ever seen? So sweet, and no mother at all. And their poor father, he's such a good man, trying to bring them up right and in that foreign city and all, don't you agree?"

DR (Trying desperately to regain control of the conversation): "Yes, yes, but what I was wondering was whether or not your viewing was interrupted during the program at all. . . ."

Mrs. KC: "Well, of course, there were those awful teenagers upstairs with their rock and roll music. I mean, a body can hardly hear herself think while they're carrying on. I do think something should be done about the young people today, don't you?"

DR: "Yes, yes, but did you leave the set at any time during the program?" (He must find out, you see, if she was actually viewing when the commercial being researched was on.)

Mrs. KC: "Why, of course not." (Is she going to tell him that she went to the bathroom twice and had a nip of the cooking sherry? And you know she didn't do either of these things while those adorable kids from Rome were on the screen.)

DR: "Then do you remember seeing a detergent commercial during *To Rome with Love?*"

Mrs. KC: "Now let me think." (Here a lot of factors come into play. To begin with, she was actually in the john when the commercial in question was on. And yet this chap on the phone seems like such a likable lad, agreeing with her on so many subjects, she'd like to help him out.) "Why yes, I do believe I did."

DR: "Fine, now can you tell me anything about the commercial?"

Mrs. KC (Now really stretching her creative powers): "Well, let me see, there was a woman (always a safe bet) and her washing machine (another sure winner)."

DR (Busily checking off his questionnaire headed "Those who remembered seeing the commercial"): "Was there anything else you remember? Do you remember what was said?"

Mrs. KC (Now warming to the challenge to her creativity): "Well, yes. There was a man, too." (She hardly deserves points for this guess either.) "And they were talking about how hard it is to get clothes clean these days." (C'mon now, Mrs. KC, have you ever seen a commercial where they weren't talking about how hard it is to get things clean?)

DR (Now ready to sign her up for good in the column headed "Remembered commercial, remembered points made, and correctly identified brand". The best list of all. The list that copywriters remember in their prayers at night.): "Now can you just tell me what the name of the detergent was?"

Mrs. KC: "Yes, it was for that new one, Burst."

Zap. Somewhere in the caverns of Madison Avenue, the Dreft copywriter lies wounded and bleeding, and another nail is pounded into the coffin of that campaign. All by a well-meaning little soul in Kansas City, too shy to admit she was heeding a call of nature when the commercial being rated was on the air, and too kind to disappoint the nice young man on the phone by telling him she couldn't remember the commercial he so obviously cared about.

It hardly bears discussion in a work on advertising, but the identical kind of research is used to decide what programs live or die. And the same kind of human frailties distort the popularity polls. That's why you and I can no longer enjoy those giggle and gasp filled hours at the tube cheering on Tuffy Brashun and Big Moose Paine on roller skates, or the Masked Marvel on the mat. None of our peers, when the dedicated researcher called, were willing to admit they were so lowbrow that they were watching either the roller derby or the wrestling matches.

This works in reverse, as well, and explains why there are reruns ad infinitum of culturally correct shows like *Civilisation* and *The Forsyte Saga*. Let's be honest with each other, now. If you were called some evening, while you were quietly getting caught up on your correspondence or contemplating your navel, by a dedicated researcher who asked what television show you were watching, assuming you did not opt for the ultimate snob statement that you were among the country's 7 per cent without a set, wouldn't you really pick a name like *The Forsyte Saga* or *Civilisation* rather than wrestling? Well, out in Numbersland, way out west beyond the Hudson, when you're name dropping, you drop names like Lucille Ball, big Hoss, and Ed Sullivan.

I am currently working for a company that does an annual business of over $700 million and spends close to thirteen million dollars in advertising. So you know they can't be doing too many things wrong or offending too many people. But with the millions of dollars of expertise behind every advertising decision they make, everything still hits the fan when a consumer out in Kankakee writes the president (why do they always have to write the president?) that she finds too much nudity in their ads, or is offended by some other personal hangup.

If you care about the commercials you see, and want to discourage the ones you hate, here are a few suggestions I've developed from years of trying to beat or at least survive the system. When the nice man calls up and wants to know if you remember his detergent commercial, say yes and describe your favorite commercial for a competing product. If you don't happen to have a favorite detergent commercial, don't fret, many of us don't. In that case, simply describe the one you find most offensive and then deliver the *coup de grâce* to it by identifying the wrong product to the researcher at the end. If you want to take action and not wait for the dedicated researcher to call you, the most constructive thing you can do— and I mean really constructive—is to sit down at your typewriter and dash off a note to the manufacturer who is running an offensive commercial. I told you how those letters shake things up.

A different ploy works for a commercial you really like. Letters to a sponsor telling how much you're enjoying his commercials bring joy to the sponsor's heart only when his sales are on the upswing. If a sales curve is having a sinking spell, all the flattery in the world probably won't save the commercials. It can even have a reverse effect, as a matter of fact. If you're not buying his beer, he's not too happy about spending all his commercial dollars just to amuse you. How do you think he feels, with you sitting in front of your TV every night, giggling at his spots over the foam of his competitor's brew? If you really love a commercial, get out there and buy. Listen, if we'd all filled our basements with Piels back then, we'd proba-bly still be sitting around laughing and chuckling at those de-lightful Piel Brothers commercials.

The age of the consumer is upon us. Manufacturers are lis-tening—they've got to now. Either they respond to you or they'll hear it from the Feds. Just remember, though, before you fire up to defend or berate a commercial or an ad: The people who pay for it judge it by standards other than yours. They don't want to know how many people laughed at it or loved it; they're interested in how many people were moved by it to go out and put their money down.

CHAPTER XIV

I Never Called It a Cure

Back in the good old days when hucksters were first getting their sullied reputations, a man could stand on the back end of a wagon and pitch a snake oil with promises that would not only make your hair stand on end but restore it if you were bald. The early huckster could literally promise them anything, providing he had a fast enough horse for his getaway.

To see how really far we've come, all you have to do is glance through the ads in an old time magazine or look at the turn-of-the-century Sears Roebuck catalogues. In the section on patent medicines, they've pills and potions that'll cure everything from baldness and alcoholism to brain fever, nervous disorders, and weak spells. No wonder we always think of our grandfather's as a far healthier generation. With cures for everything as near as your mail-order catalogue, who wouldn't be healthy? Lydia Pinkham's pink pills for pale people may be the only ones we still see on the druggist's shelves from that age, but in her prime, Miss Pinkham was surrounded on the shelves by a mind-blowing assortment of pills and tonics. In the country's pure days of pioneering, you could sell firewater in Dry Gulch that had just wiped out half the town of Little

Creek and there was no restraint put on you—governmental or otherwise.

But we've come a long way from those marvelously unfettered days, where the claims made for any product were limited only by the huckster's imagination.

Back in the 1930's, it was the government that made the first steps toward regulating the claims an advertiser could make; the FTC and the FCC both got into the act. There was also a certain amount of industry self-regulation, and a consumer was pretty safe in believing what he heard or read in ads—providing he looked and listened carefully. There were a few cases against some companies where the government cried foul and the advertiser said it was not deceit or dishonesty but merely dramatic license, especially with the advent of TV. Little discrepancies, the companies claimed, were forced on them by the medium. Such a case might be the sandpaper shaving demonstrations that proved to be phony. But who could care less, since the amount of shaving cream sold for the purposes of shaving sandpaper just has to be miniscule.

Even these eagle-eyed branches of government, ever alert to the public weal, were not tough enough for today's crop of anti-establishmentarians. Between Nader's Raiders and Banzhaf's Bandits, you can barely make a positive statement of fact about your client's product without looking nervously over your shoulder.

Nader's Raiders, a devoted group of youngsters who evidently lie awake nights worrying about the public safety, have not only gone directly after the manufacturers—their initial targets—but are now going after the advertisements themselves. Evidently, they now feel that there is just as much danger of being severely maimed by exaggeration as by faulty construction of cars.

135

Banzhaf's Bandits, a group of activist law students of George Washington University, actually regard advertising as a far greater influence on the public than do any of its most enthusiastic practitioners along Madison Avenue. When they discovered that Campbell Soup had slipped some marbles under its veggies for photography purposes, they were up in arms. What began as a simple little homework project for a law class at GWU has burgeoned into a whole series of legal entanglements and suits that show no sign of ending. They made SOUP (Students Opposed to Unfair Practices) a household word.

Any lady who's ever ladled out a bowl of soup knows you've got to have the eye of an eagle and the steadiness of a surgeon to give every portion the same amount of solids. Short of sticking to consommés or cream soups all the time, it is almost impossible to guarantee that each hungry face at the table will have the exact same number of noodles, peas, or whatever is lying in the bottom of the soup kettle that day. So you can imagine the yawns it caused out there in Homemakerland when the lads from GWU broke the news that Campbell was propping up its vegetable soup with marbles. If you've ever served a bowl of soup, you know it never looked like any picture. All it takes is a quick flip through the pages of *McCall's* or *Good Housekeeping* to see that what's in the mind's eye of American homemakers and what's on their tables are light years apart. As a matter of fact, I kind of like to think that all those exquisite calorie-laden splendors are actually the work of the *papier mâché* maven and not some cook more adept at all that than I could ever be. But Banzhaf's Bandits feel that if you're going to see the smile, you're going to have to see the warts as well. Now the measuring and affidaviting that goes on at a soup photography session is unbelievable. But you better believe that what you see on the page is what you'll see in your kitchen—*if* you've got a kitchen equipped with the same careful measuring devices that science has provided on the set. Talk about a tempest in a teapot! Wouldn't you just love to know how some law student in the ivory-towered protection of the GWU campus got hold of the information that there *were* marbles in the bottom of the soup bowls? (And wouldn't you love to hear Bea Lillie's version of "Fairies in the Bottom of My Garden" with new lyrics along those lines?)

When the company was first accused, their initial reaction was: What marbles? This was followed by a tendency to disavow any knowledge of what those big city slickers up on Madison Avenue were doing. This really proved to be a laugh since the account had come with all the directions—learned by the previous agency—for bringing out the best when soup was being photographed. I mean you can't be in the soup business all those years without learning ways to make the product look good on camera. These guys know as much about bringing out the blush on the cheek of a tomato as the Bachrach boys know about flattering brides and businessmen. Bachrach just makes worry lines look like lines of character. What's wrong with that?

It's like the little game we used to play on *The $64,000 Question* when we had live commercials. If there was any little exaggeration the Feds felt would be hard to justify, a good portion of the viewing public would have already seen it before the sponsor was notified to cease and desist on that claim. The client's retort was a near classic. "Gosh," he'd say, all boyish innocence, "I'm sorry. You know I never got to see that commercial till we were at the studio that night." And funny thing, he always had at least one of his staff standing at the back of the theater with him when he looked at the commercial. Maybe it wasn't the first time he'd seen it, but he always put on a good show.

Now, of course, the youngsters who are dragging everyone into court for implication, innuendo, or whatever are not satisfied with a cease and desist order. Now they want an advertiser whose claims have been found fraudulent or exaggerated to devote one-quarter of his advertising space or time for at least a year to the disclosure of the FTC's ruling against them. These latest steps forward are bringing us all a lot closer to those fun-filled days in Salem.

By the time this book is published there's no telling to what excesses the government agencies, egged on by these malcontent kids, will have gone. It was recently reported in the *Times* that the FTC found the ads for three toys and Zerex deceptive. Just from reading the report in the paper, the Fed's claims of deception seem a lot more farfetched than the advertising involved.

Their gripe with the Zerex commercial (a nail puncturing the can of Zerex, and then the little spurts of antifreeze stopping automatically as the holes are sealed) is not that it's a phony demonstration, but that the demonstration doesn't prove that the antifreeze will really act as a sealant inside a motor under actual driving conditions. Now mind you, the Feds are not claiming that the product doesn't work under driving conditions, they're just saying that there are only four pounds of pressure per square inch on the contents of the can and up to fifteen pounds per square inch in cooling systems. They fail to acknowledge that the chances of your car's cooling system getting a hole the size of that nail hole in the can are pretty remote, too. The TV commercial is demonstrating a principle. The government feels that we should only be allowed to view the actual product working in its real surroundings. If this ruling takes hold, I don't ever want to see another sinus or stomach remedy shown, no matter how well it works. It'll be funny, though, if you've the stomach for it. I know one really big spender in that field who's going to have to find himself a new claim. The coating action that looks so soothing on the little glass stomach just doesn't happen to take place inside real stomachs according to some scientists I once worked with on an antacid account.

But to get back to the deceit the Feds feel they've stumbled on in Toyland recently. Turns out they feel the use of camera tricks and sound effects "unfairly exploits the gullibility of children." They further charge that commercials for two different toy companies "exaggerate and falsely represent" the cars' appearances and performances. The Feds go on to charge that the same camera and sound effects "convey a sense of involvement or participation which falsely represents their actual use." Inaccurate representation of speed and a false sense of involvement? C'mon! Have you ever gotten down to counter level at F.A.O. Schwartz where kids view cars and trains and other goodies? There isn't a camera in the world that can capture the look in a child's eye when he's watching these tiny racers performing on their miniature tracks. And the lens hasn't been invented that can "see" the speed and excitement of the Indy 500 captured in miniature the way these kids' eyes can.

If the government feels the commercials have given an exaggerated or imaginative view of the toys in question, maybe they've held their imaginations too tightly locked for too long. The purpose of any toy is the release and excitation of the child's powers of imagination. If we keep going in this direction long enough, we'll be having three-quarters of Lewis Carroll's classic expunged. Alice has probably remained safe in her Wonderland all these years because she probably isn't high on the reading list of most of our official keepers of the public welfare. More's the pity.

While I was writing this book, a government agency an-

139

nounced that they were going to do their best to eliminate the practice of having sports figures pitch toys and games to kids. They were especially incensed that a race car driver should be pushing toy racing cars. It was the contention of the government agency that the only suitable salesman would be an educator or a child psychologist who would know what toys a kid should have! Boy, if that idea took hold, what would happen to all those gridiron and diamond greats who are up there in front of the camera pitching everything from hair tonic to washing machines? The next underground movie you attend might well be preceded by a collection of old Wheaties the Breakfast of Champions commercials, banned by the new rules governing TV spokesmen.

But if you think the FTC can get into the act of the toy makers, you can imagine how they throw themselves—along with the FDA—into any campaigns based on nutrition or health claims. I don't mean the kind of curative claims you might make for a medicine or vitamin product, but the simpler claims you might want to make for a food product.

My first encounter with government regulations concerning food claims came when I was working on a shortening. At that time, the world was in a quandary about saturated and polyunsaturated fats. Frying was looked at askance by some of the more dedicated followers of this latest food craze. So we didn't dare say anything positive about fried foods at that time.

A friend of mine who is now working on a shortening has a really frustrating tale to tell. After years of testing and experimenting, they've proven that chicken fried in their product is actually less greasy than broiled chicken. Now there's a claim that should knock 'em off their feet. It probably would, too, if they could use it, but they can't. It's out of bounds for them, not because the claim isn't true but because it relies on a misunderstanding women hold about broiled foods being low in fat. Turns out chicken really isn't. But it is a belief so widely held that they aren't allowed to use the claim. Not only that, but when they tried the claim out on women, they absolutely refused to believe it; their misconception about broiled chicken was so strong that they couldn't bring themselves to believe a perfectly true claim. And another ad campaign went down the drain.

Surprisingly enough, I once found myself struggling to get my copy past legal minds when I worked on Knox Gelatine. It's a simple, pure kind of food that's been around since grandmother was a girl, so you'd wonder how you could get into problems with that. And it was no problem at all for a good part of their campaign because half their budget went into pushing Knox as an ingredient for recipes. (If you've never had any dealings with molded or jellied dishes you may not know it, but gelatine is the magic ingredient that holds those quivering towers of caloric confections together.) No problem selling Knox as an ingredient—just show a well-shaped dish, give the ingredients, and any cook who's ever seen the inside of a mold knows she has to use Knox Gelatine to make the thing work. The other half of their advertising was aimed at selling Knox as a drink that would strengthen your fingernails. Years ago, they'd done some clinical tests that proved that seven out of ten people who drank Knox Gelatine once a day for ninety days did grow longer stronger nails.

All their advertising was based on this research which had stood the test not only of time, but the close scrutiny of the Feds as well, and any changing of the words of the basic claim was KOd by a doctor Knox kept on the payroll just to watch out for any possible red flag words that might catch the eye of the ever-watchful government. I mean they really leaned over backwards in their conservatism. It was a reaction to a cease and desist order that was slapped on the company back in the thirties for some claims they used to make. On a tour of the plant and home offices, I was once shown some of their early advertising. It was an eye-popping, heart-stopping experience for a writer who wasn't allowed even to re-word the seven out of ten claim they'd been running as long as I could remember.

But back in the dim but fun days when the size of your claim was limited only by the speed of your getaway horse, their ads were really wild. They were making and implying claims for their product that people have now stopped making even for oysters! And the funny thing was, the advertising was making only half the claims that the users were claiming in their letters to old man Knox! They were really something. And I never see a towering molded dessert without wondering about it.

But those days are long gone, and only the yellowing cease and desist order remains. As competition forces the writer to find newer and more powerful claims for products, the government continues to close in from every side limiting what can be said, and how one can say it. If the government continues on in the direction it seems headed, and if there is no one to stop them, the commercial of the future may well look like this:

VIDEO	AUDIO
CLOSE-UP OF DISTINGUISHED BUT HARRIED LOOKING EXECUTIVE.	(EXECUTIVE ON CAMERA) Hello, I'm John Henry, president of Widgets, Incorporated.
MOVE IN FOR C-U OF WIDGET IN HIS HAND. (NB: BE SURE HIS HAND IS NOT SMALLER THAN AVERAGE INDICATING WIDGET IS LARGER THAN IT ACTUALLY IS)	We'd like you to try our widget 'cause we think we make a fine product. But then, what do we know?

142

As a matter of fact, the rulings concerning what you can and can't say have been falling like the rains of April. That plus the growing clout of consumerism is putting all the agencies on the defensive. To keep ahead, or at least abreast of what's new on the Washington scene, some agencies actually have a man planted on the Potomac. Others, members of the Association of American Advertising Agencies, have a biweekly newsletter issued by their Washington office, while others have members of their staff assigned just to keep up with the latest decrees. Y&R, to be safe, not only has a man in the capital, but also has a former FTC lawyer on staff in its legal department. Forewarned, they figure, is forearmed. And it is becoming part of the services offered by a full service agency to lead their clients through the maze of regulations that become more involved with every wind from Washington.

Knowing how enmeshed the Feds can become in the advertising of toys and foods, you just know they're going to really let themselves go when any manufacturer of a proprietary drug takes to the airwaves to proclaim the merits of his product. Dedicated scientists on the payrolls of the proprietary drug manufacturers work diligently for years in an attempt to develop a safe cure for the illnesses that mankind is heir to. And having made their breakthrough, they try it on various animals, then on their coworkers, and finally before it can be marketed at all, the government insists that it be clinically tested for varying amounts of time, depending on the nature of the drug. This is all to the good, and it is to these careful agencies and to one woman in particular that we can be thankful that a drug like Thalidomide was never permitted to be sold in this country. Far be it from me to denigrate the work of these commissioners and agencies. The outlawing of dangerous drugs is certainly a necessary function of any government.

143

But the copywriter's problem with the government comes long after the drug has been ruled safe and effective. Without that stamp of approval, no proprietary drug can be put on the market. Once having gotten the OK to sell their little pills, capsules, tablets, or ointments, you'd think it would all be smooth sailing and the claims would be left up to the imagination of the writer. This couldn't be further from the truth. Every claim is not only carefully scrutinized at the agency level by their legal department, but is then run through the legal department of the client. Then it is pre-tested again before the commercial is even made, when the storyboard is shown to the continuity departments of the networks. These are departments set up by the networks to make sure no commercials get on the air with false claims or offensive scenes in them. It is a form of self-censorship that the networks hope will stave off further policing by government agencies.

If you ever allow yourself the luxury of brooding over the obscure, you may perhaps have wondered why the headache medicines on the market never claim they cure your headache. What they all do, according to the copywriter—by way of three or four legal eagles—is "offer temporary relief from the pain or symptoms" of whatever. And any writer who has faced the challenge of peddling a tummy pacifier knows the rules of that game are just as clearcut as in the headache court. Here, too, you never cure the stomach ache. Cure is the biggest reddest flag word ever as far as the government is concerned. Only meat packers cure anything, in their estimation. What your remedy does is "offer relief from the annoying symptoms" or "help soothe the distress."

And if you've ever been caught in traffic in a crosstown bus and been driven to reading the display cards, you can't possibly have missed the classic non-claims for that famous hemorrhoid remedy. The writer has been so blocked—either by an ineffective product or equally ineffective legal advisors—from making any kind of promise of relief that, after reading the card carefully, you're almost convinced you'd be a lot better off just suffering in silence. I mean they have so hedged the claim that even a nonbeliever would get more comfort from a quick skimming of a few pages of Mary Baker Eddy.

While no single decision or ruling by itself seems too threatening to advertisers, taken as a group and with no indication of where or if they will ever end, these restrictions are beginning to rattle the cages along the Avenue. For a generation so bent on freedom, so against living within the strictures of the establishment, the governmental controls and regulations these kids are demanding are mind-boggling. The December 12, 1970 *New York Times* carried an article headlined "Nader Urges F.T.C. To Ban Ads Not Backed by Scientific Tests." Annoying? Maybe. But you might say, hardly impossible for the average manufacturer. Skip down a few paragraphs and read: "The regulation would restrict the advertisement of any product if there was 'any reasonable doubt' that it posed a health or safety hazard to users or an environmental health or safety hazard to the general public." Right away you have eliminated all advertising for cars, airlines, sweets (according to the ADA), and detergents. There is practically nothing on earth that can't prove dangerous in its misuse. Where then do these youngsters draw the line?

CHAPTER XV

They're Not All Difficult . . . Some Are Impossible

In a lot of ways, clients are like husbands: Good ones give you a warm, secure feeling and love you and what you're doing for them; the best ones are rich and faithful. There's nothing better than a good one and nothing worse than a bad one. It must be a fairly accurate analogy, because lovelies who carry it to its ultimate conclusion on the mattress seem to be among the most successful ladies of the Avenue.

Then, too, there's a temptation to make the same mistake in judging clients that some women make in judging husbands: They use their bankrolls as a criterion. That's not always an accurate measuring stick. The small spender can give you as many headaches as a really big one. It's just that you're usually working with the top man in the company when a small budget's involved. Never having worked for a small agency, or one that accepted really small accounts, I've never had the pleasure of working with a client with a tiny budget. But some of my friends have and they're all convinced, the smaller the budget, the bigger the headaches.

What does seem to me to be a rule of thumb, though, is the farther away you are from the man who makes the final decision—whether he's the executive VP in charge of advertising or the president of the whole shebang—the farther you are from a happy relationship. On all too few occasions, I've worked on accounts where there was close contact between the head of the company and the copywriter. It's the greatest working relationship in the world, no matter what kind of a guy the client is. At least you're face to face with him and he's aware that you're trying just as hard to peddle his widgets as he is. You're not just some unidentified face in the bowels of the agency, sniffing glue and trying to cop awards for yourself every time there's a convention of your peers.

In the first place, these tiny tycoons are usually so spastic with joy at the thought of some bright-eyed Madison Avenue lady who really cares about their products that they're really cupcakes to deal with. That's *usually*. Back in the good old days, when I was young and impressionable, I had the opportunity to work eyeball to eyeball with one of the cosmetic giants not known for his easy ways with agencies. What he was doing at an agency like ours was hard to tell, except that TV was very new at the time, and the little chi-chi shops where he had been hopping around, making and breaking agencies at the drop of his budget, didn't have the know-how of that medium we had. And that's why he was at the granddaddy of them all. Nobody was more surprised along the Avenue than we were when this plum (or lemon, depending on whether you were judging the account by its budget or its demands) walked through the door one morning.

I remember a short pep talk given to the chosen ones who were to work with the client. It was delivered by one of the agency's grey-haired, pin-striped dignitaries. He told us that he was aware of the rather unfortunate image our new client had with agency people, and he didn't want any of us to worry

147

about that. "We're going to teach him to do business our way, not the other way around." We all relaxed and threw ourselves into the cosmetics game with high hopes.

What actually happened was that the client learned everything he thought he had to know about this exciting new medium and then whisked his account away to another agency where they'd do things his way. We never taught him how we did business, but we did breathe a sigh of relief when he took his little pots of rouge and tubes of lipsticks elsewhere.

Like everything else you have to go through, you learn how to live even with an account like that. We developed a wonderful system for showing him our commercials and believe me, we showed him plenty. He had taken to TV like a duck to water and all his commercials at the time were done live, so there were no repeats. This client had a marvelous little quirk. Whatever commercial you offered him first, he'd verbally tear it to shreds. "You call this a commercial?" was the nicest thing he'd say about it. The agency troops would stand there listening to his tirade and when he had run down, we'd hand him a second commercial with the remark, "You're right. That's why we've included all those considerations in this one."

The little game worked like a charm; the second commercial was always home free. Back at the agency, the work was divided up between another writer and myself. And we were such sticklers for fair play that each week we would take turns writing the straw men that got tossed on his desk first. It was only fair, and the week you wrote the straw men you could allow yourself some little double entendres and wordplays that were much appreciated by your co-workers and never did any harm since they were destined for the round file anyhow.

I wouldn't want to have worked on that cosmetic account an hour more than I did, but I must say the experience was worth its weight in blood, sweat, and tears. On your résumé, that account singles you out as a writer who can not only work with *any* client, but as one who's been through the trial by fire and come out unscathed. The alumni of that account could fill Shea Stadium with outrageous stories and broken campaigns. And like the men who fought in the Battle of the Bulge, there's a kind of camaraderie among them that no other account seems to bring about. I'm just glad I was as young and resilient as I was when I went through it.

But difficult as that particular client was, at least no meant no and yes meant run it. The really difficult client is the one who protects himself and his endless layers of executives from ever having to take the rap for a bad ad or campaign. This is the situation you have at all the soap companies and on most really big accounts. It's something like the Chinese water torture for a writer. Every level, and believe me, they've got more levels of responsibility than they have soap flakes, has to feel it's made a contribution to the final ad, and every level has to protect itself in case the thing really bombs. A straight answer is as hard to come by on those accounts as a straight guy in the East Fifties.

The first level consists of Harvard Business School grads who look about twelve years old and are just about that perceptive. They noodle and worry over prepositions, conjunctions, and adjectives. Because of them, I've seen agencies make that long trip to the client's as often as three or four times just to change a plus to an and. These are the moments that try a writer's soul, not the big battles with the flamboyant bully in the corner office who's as apt to spit on your layout as he is to love it.

At the next level of authority—and I use the word loosely— are the boys who have survived a few campaigns at the bottom and are beginning to climb out of anonymity. They use the ad for two things: to further their careers and to test the mettle of

149

the men under them. It's a rare commercial or ad that can live through this kind of inter-office warfare. This is also the level where they may begin to question the basic concept of the commercial. "Do we really want to position ourselves as the detergent for big families?" (Who else uses so much detergent? And after all, you're not going to have to entertain these people in your home, just sell them soap.) The esoteric nature of the questions that can come up when a guy is really just stalling for time, and trying to read the reaction of his superior without actually tipping his hand, is not to be believed. By the time a commercial for a big soaper is on the air, more people have seen it in various stages of development than will eventually view it on TV.

If any advertising is ever to run, somewhere along this peevish pecking order somebody has to OK the script or storyboard for production. But before this is done, every level along the way has so hedged its acceptance and so questioned everything about it, that if the thing should research badly, they've all got an out.

Just as nobody takes the responsibility for a bad spot, everybody takes the credit for a good one. No less frustrating, but actually a lot more fun in a sadistic kind of way, is the client whose management is on an equal level. This happens when the client is a commission or association, like the Florida Citrus Growers, the Upholstery Leather Groups, the Avocado Board, the Dairy Association, and last but not least, the Government Tourist Offices. They not only have all the usual pushing and shoving involved with these commission accounts, but they throw in the added spice of political unrest. An OK for each ad practically calls for a national referendum.

When you're writing copy for a commission or an association, everybody on the commission or association is supposed to have an equal say because they're all supposed to be equal.

But anyone with even a tentative grasp on reality knows that some commission members are created more equal than others. Lincoln never worked with a commission or he'd have rethought his remarks. I used to work on the Florida Citrus account, and you can bet your last orange pit that the owner of the fifty thousand acre grove had a much bigger voice in the advertising we ran than the guy with a dozen or so acres. This particular account was made doubly interesting because the head of the agency was dabbling both in champion cattle raising in Jersey estate territory and citrus groves in Florida. Obviously he was not a man to pass up any tax easement, and his citrus holdings made for really interesting meetings. He could actually sit on both sides of the conference table, as head honcho of the agency and member of the commission.

But whether they come in groups, behind platoons of lower echelon flunkies, or straight out of the chairman's office, all clients have certain endearing quirks that take some getting used to. A friend of mine, a young copywriter at the time, couldn't figure out for months why every single ad she sent to a certain big dairy client always came back with the verbs deleted. Finally she found out that the ad manager had come up through the ranks of the organization and had been a milkman many years before. I guess years of reading "Two qts. milk, $\frac{1}{2}$ lb. butter, no cream, thanks" really proved to him that verbs were superfluous.

One otherwise charming client I worked with had one really blind spot: He never wanted a model without a wedding ring to appear in any of his ads. He was so adamant on this point that when an art director new to the account photographed a girl without a wedding ring, we had to have an artist retouch one onto her finger! Now if you're selling diapers or contraceptives, I could see this kind of a preference. But he was selling a drink that was supposed to be good for your fingernails. Only married ladies should want long, strong nails? It used to make me wonder a lot until I visited the plant and executive offices of this client. Up there in a little Victorian hamlet in God's country, all the good women of the town were married. There really wasn't any other choice for a good woman in that town. So I guess by slipping a gold band on the model's finger he figured she'd look just like one of the girls back home.

Harder to fathom, but more fun to repeat, was the remark made by the cosmetic mogul who was in the throes of upgrading his product's image. The agency was trying to convince him that the ad—and consequently his product—would look a lot richer with lots of white space. The client, not far removed from his pushcart beginnings and used to getting a dime's worth of value out of every nickel he spent, was having trouble buying the idea. The agency remained adamant—the ad needed white space. Throwing up his hands, the client came up with a classic: "Okay, Okay. I don't mind white space . . . but does it have to be empty?"

Whatever their individual quirks, a great many clients share one big common desire above and beyond the obvious one of wanting to increase sales and profits. They all are hell-bent on telling those ladies out in Consumerland just how hard it is for them to make their widget. Although most clients today are far too sophisticated to think a picture of the plant or the founder in an ad is sure to double sales, they still cling to this desire to tell you how much trouble they went to to make their little widget better. This is especially true if the man you're dealing with has any other responsibilities above and beyond advertising. What all these hard-working men don't seem to realize is that women couldn't care less about the difficulties of product production. As a matter of fact, if you persist in belaboring the point, Mrs. Consumer is very apt to think that you're not making a better widget, you're just not good at making widgets. The kind of ad that works so well for Rolls Royce, telling of each painstaking hand done process brings yawns or surprise from women, who feel the time and effort might better have been devoted to something else.

Not only are most clients like husbands, but most clients *are* husbands and that brings another genus into the advertising jungle: the client's wife. If there is one voice above all others that rings out through the halls of Madison Avenue, it is the voice of the client's wife. Some clients have the decency to cloak her sentiments and opinions and spout them as their own, but once you get to know a client at all well, he's sure to slip it to you straight: "Just last night, my wife suggested . . ." or "My wife thinks we should. . . ." If those women's lib ladies had their heads screwed on right and really wanted to make their feelings felt, they'd all marry clients. It may not be the *only* way to be heard—but it sure is one way. Naturally they're not all bad, but then again, they're not all that helpful to a besieged writer, either.

A friend of mine on a diet cola account was just about home free with a storyboard that was about to be made into a really great commercial, lots of tongue in cheek humor, delightful situations, each scene a telling little vignette, and each beautifully cast. Getting a commercial like this OKd is as hard as getting five or six one-situation commercials past muster. Each vignette had been thoroughly gone over by everybody from the head bubble at the cola plant to the sweep-up guy.

It was at that breathe-easy stage prior to filming and my friend was leaning back ever so lightly on her laurels when the client blew into town to show the little woman some of the sights of the big city. On top of the usual tourist attractions, he figured she'd like a peek at the agency.

She came sweeping into the office one afternoon, all

153

Blanche DuBois costuming and corn pone dripping from her lips. She was shown the spot's storyboard, and my friend almost suffered a cardiac arrest when this Southern belle said she thought the board was such a pretty thing they ought to just show that on the air and not spend all that money having it produced on film! Then she was shown pictures of the actors and actresses who had been chosen for the spot. "Course ah know nothin' 'bout advertisin'," she drawled, "but actin' is somethin' else. I've had mah share of that!" *He* at least had the decency to blush. "My wife is quite a star in our local little theater group," he explained. Fortunately, before there was any move to find a role suitable for her talents in the spot, the account man hustled them out of the office.

The classic client with the talented wife is the coffeemaker who insists on having his wife sing and star in his television spots. Actually it's not as big a bore as you might expect, since he's been through a series of wives. Despite the variety of this talent, one can easily imagine the agency producer or casting director wishing fervently that the coffee king would think about how she'll look singing along with a can of coffee in her hand before he slips the gold band on the next fragile finger.

An account man will tell you that nobody knows the client as well as he does, and a copywriter often will claim the same inner knowledge. But some clients you can get to know without even working in the business. When you see an account the size of Alka Seltzer bouncing around from agency to agency, after getting some of the best advertising on the air from their agencies, you've got a pretty good idea of the kind of mind operating there. Who can forget those spots done for Alka Seltzer by Doyle Dane (the marshmallowed meatball bride and the spicy meatball actor)? That account had the very best creative minds at that agency working on it. Having tried their favors, the client is now off to another shop to taste theirs. On Main Street, USA, when a guy like that is loose, mothers lock up their daughters. But along Madison Avenue when a guy with over twenty million a year to spend comes along, the red carpet's out at every door.

CHAPTER XVI

Ready Whenever You Are, C.B.

The same client who wouldn't be caught dead trooping over to the studio to see some virtuoso of the still camera photograph his product, would walk barefoot on hot coals to be present at the shooting of one of his TV spots. These little epics run in length from an eight-second ID (those little commerical flashes you see in combination with station breaks) to ninety-second spectaculars. These are rare since the client has to own a pretty big part of a pretty big show to have this much commercial time at his disposal.

The cost of these little films can run as high as $130,000 which is just about twice the amount of money it took to produce some of those French nouvelle vague features that came out of France during the 50's. So when you realize how much every golden frame is costing the client, you can appreciate his interest in the whole production. Understanding it is one thing, coping with it is another.

I'm convinced that deep in the heart of every man who whiles away his working hours making or peddling soap, deodorants, or tires, is the dream of being a Hollywood director or producer. For every little girl who grows up wanting to be a movie star, there have to be at least a dozen little boys growing up with the hidden ambition of being another DeMille. Owing to pressures in the social system too deep to go into here, most of these lads have sublimated this desire by the time they leave their teens. But as any psychiatrist worth his couch knows, a desire sublimated is a desire to be coped with—eventually. And that's what most agencies are paid to do: cope.

The closest most men ever come to directing a multi-million-dollar epic is throwing their weight around on the tiny set where their commercial is being shot.

While I have never actually seen a client show up for one of these little festivities with a vicuña coat thrown over his shoulders and a riding crop to slap against his leather puttees, you just know that under that pin-striped suit beats the heart of a frustrated Fellini, who sees himself more moviemaker than marketing man.

If the client is a relatively small one (a truly small one could never even dream of entering the heady and outrageously expensive world of Videoland to begin with), the man who shows up is usually the president of the company or the ad manager. Now obviously the agency wouldn't dream of allowing their precious client loose on the set with just the creative and production types from the agency. Left to their own devices they'd probably blow the whole account, the agency moguls reason. So on top of the agency art director, producer, and writer, you have at least one account executive. If the account is big enough, an account supervisor or even a management supervisor might show up. It is the job of these stalwarts to stand between the client and any harm—physical or psychological—which might come from contact with falling cables or temperamental directors.

Because there is always a script girl, usually a home economist or two, a stylist, and often a model who will appear in the commercial, the set is far from a male preserve. Still, the number of females from the agency is usually quite limited. Agency producers resent the presence of the writer on the set because they feel it limits their contribution to the finished commercial. (This contribution is known affectionately among writers as "lousing it up.") So the agency hardly ever has a female on the set except for a really determined copywriter or—that even rarer exception—the lady producer. A friend of mine, Joan Dunne, who was one of those rare birds, was finally driven from the ranks of producer to writer. Every time she showed up on the set someone who couldn't believe such a sweet young thing could be a producer would send her out for coffee!

That may be one of the reasons the only lady producer I ever worked with, Anne Bachner, carried her own mug of coffee with her wherever she went. If she ever leaves TV production, she'll probably have to have it removed from her hand surgically. Anyhow, she was a delight to work with, never spilled a drop, and never forgot one of the incredible number of details an agency producer must carry around in her head. But these ladies were real exceptions.

Lady producers at the production houses are an even rarer breed. My friend Anne, though, did eventually make the move from agency to production house as a director. (She now is a freelance director—the first lady to win the Lion d'Or at the Cannes Film Festival.) Once you make this move you usually have to become a member of one of the unions involved, IATSE or NABET.

The International Alliance of Theatrical and Stage Employees is the more demanding of the two and larger than the National Association of Broadcast Employees and Technicians. Either way, these are the folks who really make for a crowded set. They feel the simplest little :08 ID has to be staffed and crewed as lavishly as the most elaborate production ever put on film.

Their idea of a minimum crew to handle an eight-second film spot showing a box of cereal and maybe a bowl staggers the imagination. *Birth of a Nation* was probably photographed with a smaller crew. There's a prop man who moves the product onto the set, a set decorator or stylist who has picked out the bowl; there are grips whose sole function is to move anything larger than a prop (How do you think the table, the box, and the bowl got there?); there are electricians, an assistant cameraman, a cameraman, a director, a producer. . . . And if, God forbid, your commercial should require the presence on screen of a living human being or any portion of same, there's the makeup man, the hairdresser, the stylist.

None of these specialists is out there earning coolie wages. The pay ranges from $40 a day up to $1,000 or more. You can imagine what that does to the cost of your little commercial. It'll probably come as no surprise that the lowest salary on the set goes with a job (production assistant) invariably held by a woman, and the top dollar to a director, just as invariably a man.

In the early 1960's when union demands started skyrocketing, a lot of Hollywood moviemakers packed up their scripts and stars and went off to the far corners of the world to make their movies beyond the jurisdiction of the unions. It became cheaper to shoot on location than to fake it on the back lot. Commercial producers took a page from the big guys and followed them out of the country. This was known as runaway production and was loathed by the unions but loved by the clients. It made financial sense, which is hard to argue with, and it gave the agency and client personnel the chance to fly now, pay never. But all *that* exotica is in another chapter. Here, we'll stick to NY production.

With the advent of tape, it's hard now to find a show, let alone a commercial, that is done live, and so a lot of the fun of watching early television is gone. Any boo-boo you find an announcer making in a commercial now has undoubtedly been OKd by close to fifty people and probably been rehearsed for hours. But when I began writing commercials, a great many of them, as well as the shows, were done live. Then, each commercial had some of the excitement of a mini-Broadway opening.

I'll never forget the first live commercial I had to cover. It was for a pudding. The commercial was to appear on an afternoon variety show which originated from the stage of one of those Broadway theaters that had happened on sorry times. Anyhow, it was a richly baroque affair and the endless cables, lights, and other TV impedimenta seemed ill at ease in the surroundings. They had nothing on me, however. I was new enough in advertising to have a sharply defined list of rules in my head. One of them was that the product should dominate the screen. This isn't always easy.

No matter what the average homemaker serves her pudding in, we at BBDO always showed pudding in those little glass dishes that could pinch hit for champagne glasses. Next to one of these, the package was more than able to hold its own, and the dessert itself looked pretty impressive—assuming of course you had the camera lens within inches of the product. In rehearsal we'd seen wonderfully enormous shots of dishes of chocolate and vanilla pudding which, if not mouthwatering in glorious black and white, were at least impressive looking in their screen-filling size.

We had run through the camera movements of the commercial a couple of times rather quickly, without benefit of the star who was to do the pitch, and all seemed well. (The star was

Kate Smith who was emceeing her own show!) Well, when the time came for the actual broadcast, there was our little dish of pudding next to its little box—all directly in front of the rather impressive expanse of Miss Smith. When the camera included any recognizable portions of Miss Smith, our product was almost invisible, and when the product dominated the scene, you can imagine just how much of Miss Smith we could see.

Sitting in the back row of the darkened and almost deserted theater as the show went on the air was a profoundly moving experience for me. The client joined me in this moment of truth and as soon as his contract ran out, he went off TV until he could make up some film spots.

Sometimes in those days of live production, the very restrictions and limitations of the medium forced you into some good ideas. When I was writing the live Betty Crocker commercials for the Robert Q. Lewis show, we needed a prop and setting that would work well as a commercial area and could easily be identified as Betty Crocker's. The art director suggested an early American hutch (what could be homier?) as an excellent place to show off both our packages and our cakes. I suggested the wooden spoon for a prop and a trademark. The handle was marked off in inches to measure the height of our cakes (height—not moisture—was the big thing in those days), and the bowl of the spoon was painted on the door of the hutch, a constant identifying mark. That red spoon trademark eventually made its way onto all Betty Crocker packages and is still being used. Too bad you don't get residuals for ideas.

Owing to the presence of an extra chromosome in my genetic structure, I have been assigned to push so-called women's products throughout most of my life in Adland. The depth of agency thinking on this subject is really impressive: Women were to write on women's products and men were to write on men's products. But owing to what the agencies consider a natural balance of things, there were always more men writers than women writers and, oddly enough, more women's products than men's. That's why many men were assigned to women's products, but the reverse was hardly ever true.

Despite the gargantuan efforts of women's lib to set all this straight, it is still pretty much true today, although the line is not as strictly held as it was just a few years ago when a woman would never be asked to write on a cigarette or—heaven forfend—a booze account. It was a nice little Victorian touch in an otherwise pseudo-sophisticated world, I thought, and I hated to see it pass—mostly because I had little or nothing to say about the advantages of cigarettes, and my feelings toward booze were too personal to document in four color spreads in *Life*.

This all leads up to the fact that many of my efforts through the years have been devoted to hustling food. And I must admit as a dedicated nosher, many of my happiest moments were spent nibbling my way around the set. Very carefully, I might add, for until recently, when the government got really sticky about truth in advertising and no substitutes could be used for food shots, you could find yourself nibbling on some rather unusual things. In the case of the pudding mentioned earlier, the dollop of whipped cream on top was actually shaving cream. It held up much better under the hot lights of the set than did real whipped cream.

With the passing of live commercials, a lot of these substitutions were no longer necessary, although long after film and tape arrived, things like stand-in cakes were always baked and carefully prepared for use during the seemingly endless camera rehearsals. Just as the camera was about to roll, a home economist, who had been poking away with a toothpick "texturizing" the cake which was to eventually star in the commercial, would whisk away the stand-in cake and replace it with the carefully worked-over star.

To get one star cake for a commercial, Grace Manning and her assistants in the BBDO kitchen would often bake as many as a half dozen stand-ins. God forbid you should gather all that expensive talent only to watch your star have a sinking spell right in the middle of one of its layers! Grace has since gone into her own business as a TV food specialist and is finally reaping some of the rewards she so justly deserves.

The women who labor so long, unseen and unsung, lavishing expertise and loving care over the dishes you see some bright-eyed little model set proudly on the table, deserve the undying gratitude of the clients and all those ravenous set bums who devour everything in sight the moment it comes off camera.

One of the most unforgettable moments in a long career of peddling food occurred in the screening room at Benton & Bowles where we were screening the rushes on a cake commercial for a shortening we had at that time.

Assigned to this particular product was one of those endless middle-management guys who was working his way up the corporate structure through the glamorous end of the business: second-guessing the television commercial producers. Anyhow, by the time our paths crossed he was fairly well along the ladder, and he had done it all on the strength of one shot. He claimed he had invented it, and he was using it to grease his way to the top. It was the embarrassingly tight ECU (Extreme Close-Up) of a piece of cake. You must remember the shot: When the fork came into the scene to dig into the cake, its tines practically reached across the screen. From this perspective, of course, you got an unnecessarily good look at the actual texture of the cake. (On this his career was built? But no matter.)

163

Since he was newly arrived on our account, he was indoctrinating the troops in the method and psychology of the shot. The tiny screening room was chockablock full of eager agency types. After the footage of our commercials was run off, he ran some of *his* shots from other cake commercials he had masterminded. It was turning into a gourmand's film festival. The dialogue—or rather monologue—in the darkened room was not to be believed:

VIDEO	AUDIO
SCREEN-FILLING SHOT OF A SINGLE PIECE OF FROSTED TWO-LAYER CAKE LYING ON ITS SIDE ON A SMALL PLATE. CAMERA MOVES IN FOR CLOSER SHOT.	(THE CAKE MAVEN:) "Here, of course, you see the virgin piece."
	"Now we are becoming more intimate with the piece. Here the danger is that we become too intimate too quickly. The camera must pause here . . . almost shyly." (Several nervous coughs from agency personnel.)
ON AN ECU, THE TINES OF THE FORK ENTER THE SCENE, AND BREAK INTO THE PIECE OF CAKE.	"Now we see the assault on the virgin piece."
THE TINES OF THE FORK LIFT A SMALL BITE-SIZE PIECE OF CAKE UP AND OFF CAMERA. A LITTLE BIT OF FROSTING CLINGS TO THE FORK A MOMENT BEFORE CURLING BACK DOWN ONTO THE CAKE.	(More nervous coughing.) "Now the withdrawal. Nothing hurried about it, slooow—so the viewer's anticipation grows."
CUT TO CU PACKAGE OF CAKE MIX. LIGHTS IN THE SCREENING ROOM GO ON.	"You do see what I have in mind, don't you?"

The meeting broke up shortly after this and one agency man went right to his office and phoned his psychiatrist. Two things resulted from that screening: A serving of cake was thereafter always called a wedge, not a piece and anyone who had been at the screening from then on referred to it as the "Rape of the Cake" screening.

But life in Adland wasn't always a piece of cake. Long before TV was perfected to the point it is now and you can have your people on screen in a wide range of unearthly colors, the cosmetic people had discovered the power of the medium and were swarming to it. Most of them waited to make the plunge until the days of live TV were over. It was lucky in one case.

A friend of mine was the producer of television commercials for Helena Rubinstein who thought TV would be the perfect place to introduce their new waterproof mascara. Back at their labs they'd tested it on models who had cried copiously and stood under showers for ages. So they were sure they were ready. To prove that the mascara wouldn't run under emotional or elemental stress, the commercial was to show a pretty young thing dive into a pool and come up to the camera with every eyelash dark and lustrous and no trace of mascara anywhere else on her face.

There was the usual retinue of agency, client, and production lackeys on hand for the filming. All went well until the model made her first dive. She surfaced looking a lot like Al Jolson made up to sing "Mammy." The scene poolside became extremely ugly with wild accusations flying around, including one that the model agency had deliberately sent a girl with defective eyelashes! But when cooler heads finally prevailed, it was decided that the chemicals in the pool had made the mascara run. Since most girls spend more time in pools than in tears, it was back to the drawing boards at the labs. And be-

165

fore the product was finally marketed, it was made water-proof.

In advertising circles when they speak of cleanliness being next to godliness, you should realize they mean next to and just a little bit in front of God. That's because soaps and detergents are such big spenders—especially when compared to the amount God spends.

One of the biggest users of TV spots during its introductory stage was Zest. For any tots out there whose viewing habits started after Zest was discovered, let me just say that their line was "For the first time in your life—feel really clean!" That message was driven home in a series of excitingly-filmed commercials showing people diving into the surf or dropping into pools from the trees. A hard-pounding jingle and some hard sell words were added, plus some interior shots of people lathering it up in the tub and shower. These commercials all came out long before cigarettes, toothpastes, and feminine deodorants took over the waterfront. In those days, the beach belonged to Zest. So did the high-speed photography which slowed down the action giving the viewer more of a chance to enjoy the sensation of plunging into the surf. All exterior shots were done on location, of course, since you couldn't expect models to frolic in the surf during February at Coney Island. A lot of agency time was spent on tropical beaches recording the watery activities with a cameraman named Johnny Ercole, a whiz who had a specially rigged camera that would allow him to follow the action into some of the most breathtaking surf this side of Hawaii.

But since I was low man on the creative totem pole at that time, I was sent to cover only the indoor shootings which were done in the West Fifties. Don't think that neighborhood didn't have its exciting moments. One in particular was an electrifying experience.

Half a day had been spent setting up the shot of a lovely tucked into a tub of suds center stage. Cables, clients, and crew were strewn all over the set. One highly trained member of the crew had dumped a box of detergent into the tub and with an electric beater was whipping up a storm of suds that were supposed to keep the commercial from getting an X rating. Anyhow, at the time of crisis there he was at one end of the tub with his egg beater, and there she was at the other end, up to her armpits in suds. Surrounding this ill-matched pair were all the lights, camera, crew, agency, and client personnel that seem to be regulation under the circumstances.

The client, who had arrived a little late, kept asking if the model had on a bathing suit. He was getting all kinds of arch answers (gotta keep the client happy and interested—no matter what). Most of us were standing around in little puddles of water that had been spilled in filling the tub.

The cameraman was rolling in on the dolly to frame the shot for the CU when a loud noise and a flash of sparks from one of the cables twisting through the puddles on the floor indicated that all was not as Edison had planned. "Freeze!" yelled the producer, and what had been a busy, noisy set an instant before looked like a still from an Antonioni film. The only sound that could be heard was the whirring of the egg beater. The producer yelled for someone in the corner of the stage to pull the main power switch. Just before the place blacked out, the model suddenly realized the danger she was in and stood up in the tub. The only movement on the crowded set in that moment was the almost imperceptible widening of the pupils of the client's eyes when he finally got the answer to his question, did she or didn't she.

CHAPTER XVII

Around the World in Ninety Seconds

Young girls with a penchant for travel, and no desire to see the world over a pile of plastic airline trays, might be well-advised to consider the Avenue as a way of life. Advertising became a viable alternative to airline service the moment filmed spots replaced the live, in-studio commercials. Writers and producers as well as art directors were quick to see the advantage of setting a commercial on a sunny beach if it was to be filmed mid-winter, or on a Parisian street corner or next to a Roman fountain any time of the year.

A writer with any creativity at all could write his favorite locale or sport into a commercial for practically any product. Writers who adored skiing, but found the weekend assaults on New England financially as well as physically draining, merely wrote a ski scene into whatever commercial happened to be in their typewriters at the time. If you've ever wondered why a camera crew of ten, plus the models and all the agency and client personnel had to be dragged out to Aspen merely to record the model's dazzling smile, the coolness of a cigarette, or the efficacy of a deodorant soap, now you know. After a year or two of this, your sample reel gave away almost as much about your avocations as it did about your ability to write.

Reputations were made and broken in this way. Any writer known for an ability to work an exotic background into a sales pitch was adored by art directors and producers alike. Don't think *they* don't enjoy a little time away from the office, too. And since the account man as well as the client was included in these little safaris, there was really no one to call a halt to the general exodus.

Travel departments in the bigger agencies, used to booking only round trip, overnight flights to places like Akron and Minneapolis, took on the ambiance of your friendly neighborhood Cook's office. Across their desks came requisitions for tickets to and accommodations in such widely separated spots as Acapulco, Aspen, the Alps, and Zanzibar. No matter how outrageously expensive and exotic the trip, though, if the crew comes back with super commercials, all seems to be forgiven immediately.

You can imagine the chagrin of the Maclean's team when they came back from a Caribbean boondoggle empty-handed. It wasn't really their fault, but it was embarrassing. Despite all the red tape and difficulties the black government had put in their way, the crew had managed to get all their equipment and film released from the Customs warehouse. The group was assembled poolside the first morning having breakfast when the news came. The model whose faultless smile was to be featured had eloped the night before, and she was sorry, of course, but she wouldn't be able to join them in Nassau. She gave, as the excuse, that she had a bad cold—which seems a funny way to describe it.

It was Easter week and the pool was crowded with lithe, leggy, All-American beauties with builds and smiles that were breathtaking. But the client, who had inadvertently been left home, wouldn't agree to let the agency team substitute another girl. So the entire group kicked the sand out of their espadrilles and lenses and took the next plane back to New York. Now you know why you must *never* leave the client home.

Airline and government tourist accounts are widely favored and the competition to work on them is fierce. For one thing, there isn't the slightest need to excuse or explain commercials with foreign settings. The account requires it. And for another thing, there is always enough free travel on these accounts so that there is little or no jealousy among co-workers who would not otherwise be included on location shooting trips. If you've ever wondered why so much airline advertising shows destinations rather than the insides of airports, hangars, or aircraft, remember: It's a rare copywriter who gets any kick out of airports, hangars, or jet interiors.

Undoubtedly one of the most imaginative uses of location shooting came from an agency in midtown Manhattan. At the time, they had a cookie account and the commercial called for a close-up of a freckle-faced kid enjoying the product. The announcer was to give the spiel while the kid contentedly munched away. Easiest kind of commercial in the world to shoot: no background showed, no long establishing shot, no set necessary; the kid's face just about filled the screen. Kind of a tot's version of that great eat, eat, and enjoy scene from *Tom Jones*. Could have been shot in any closet in town, right? Wrong. Would you believe the agency producer huddled with the film producer and came up with a trip to Ireland!

The reasoning, if you can call it that, was: As long as we're after a cute, freckled-faced kid, let's go someplace where cute, freckled-faced kids abound. Where else? All you mothers of cute, freckle-faced kids can just start seething quietly. Kind of an ironic footnote to the whole episode was provided by the United States Customs department who impounded the film's negative and insisted it be developed before they'd release it. They were that sure it was pornographic! A cookie commercial shot in Ireland?

Wanderlust must be inborn in copywriters. Even those in Europe have the travel bug. An American expatriate who now is a partner in one of the very hottest creative shops in London is a classic example. A few years ago I was doing the beach, bar, boutique beat in the Bahamas when I ran into him. Accompanied by the traveling circus that makes up a production crew, he had come to Nassau from England to shoot a couple of candy bar commercials! Now don't tell me the English aren't an imaginative crowd. And never assume that the copywriter's best creative effort is lavished on the script; it often goes into the pre-production meeting when trips like these are made to seem necessary.

Though American copywriters seem to feel Europe is the perfect setting for selling anything, European writers never seem to be happy shooting on their native soil. London copywriters shoot in Holland, Belgian writers in London, and sooner or later almost all European writers shoot in Germany. Berlin seems to be the best place for that, and on the sets there you'll find a lot of the old mystique that was part of the Eric von Stroheim school of film making. The cameraman is always *Herr*—no first names please. German vodka is served mid-afternoon, and throughout the shooting day beer flows constantly, replacing the ubiquitous coffee in containers on the American scene.

A friend of mine writing in Belgium found herself chaperoning half a dozen Dutch housewife types to London to shoot a P&G commercial. She was dismayed to discover that for every woman she had to obtain written consent of the husband

171

before any of these ladies would dream of leaving hearth and home. Now let's hear it from all those outraged women's lib members.

Of course, once the film production houses realized how popular these little guided tours were with both agency and client personnel, they began including the price of the trip in their initial bids. Popular indeed was the producer who for supposedly aesthetic reasons insisted on authenticity of locale and still brought in a competitive bid. It was a rare commercial producer who didn't each year travel at least as much as the company that filmed "Around the World in Eighty Days." The hand-held Arriflex camera made location shooting both feasible and a lot less expensive.

Tabletop product shots which took hours to light on a soundstage in town were accomplished in minutes on location. Products were shown being washed up on shore by the surf, sticking out of snowbanks, and tucked into a crevice in a Bernini fountain. And if, in the excitement of the trip, the product shot was inadvertently overlooked, back home in the labs on the West Side the product could be optically superimposed over some of the excess footage—and there is invariably enough excess footage to put together a small feature.

I know one writer who saved enough money by using his location jaunts in lieu of vacations to be able to buy a house on Fire Island. His wife rather missed their holiday trips together, but she's now quite fond of their beach house. Wives and husbands are not usually included in these little trips. Lovers . . . that's another story.

Since the general tone of these junkets is one of schoolboys on an unexpected holiday, there is almost never a self-appointed keeper of the group morals. Live and let live—and as high on the hog as the budget will allow—is the order of the day. If anyone is having a thing with one of the models, there is no one to point the finger of guilt or shame. Next time there's always the chance the model will be having a thing with you.

It's a shortsighted model who casts her favors toward any member of the production house. The model who knows which side her residuals are buttered on, devotes her off-camera attention to the client or at least to the agency account man, for these are the men who have the final say on who will star in the account's next epic.

With everyone on location looking the other way, you might think these little traveling affairs go undetected and unpunished. A lot of them do, of course. But a couple I know of had some wide-ranging results. Oddly enough, in both cases it was some little gnome in the client's accounting department who blew the whistle.

The first jaunt was one to photograph a soap commercial. It had originally been scheduled to be shot in Florida, but owing to what the Chamber of Commerce referred to as highly unusual weather—rain—the action had been shifted to the Bahamas. Because of the last minute switch in location, the usually leisurely location hunt had to be speeded up considerably. This is probably why the beach picked as the ideal spot turned out to be the private preserve of the island's Governor General.

The Guv came home from a hard day at Government House, prepared for a quiet dip, and found a small army of Americans had taken over his beach. He made the expected irate sounds which were duly reported in the Nassau press. On that island anything more exciting than the tides coming and going amounts to a real news break. A man very high on the P&G pecking order just happened to be vacationing in Nassau when all this happened. Ever aware of the soft spot the English have in their hearts for Unilever, he rushed into the breach with a flurry of apologies and a promise to investigate the whole unpleasant affair. No sooner was he back in Suds City than the memos began to fly. Bad enough they had commandeered the Governor's beach; but the investigation was of such a nitty-gritty nature that it turned up the fact that one of the models, whose entire footage had been shot the first day, was bedded and boarded for the entire *week* in Nassau on the production budget, solely for the delectation of a member of the production staff.

For companies that push clean as a way of life, it must be an unfortunate coincidence that the other little bedroom farce occurred on the location of a detergent spot. The agency had sent its top creative gun to cover the filming of the first in a series of spots for this account. There was really big money involved, and that's why the creative director went along.

Off they went to Miami to grab off a little sunshine and open some new advertising frontiers. Back in the office remained a copywriter who had been sharing the copy director's bed but not this particular account. Without the creative director to run interference for her, she began taking a little more flak than she could handle. Without a word to anyone in the office, she walked out of a meeting one day and got on a plane for Miami for the kind of reassurance a girl can only get from her creative director. She tucked herself into his motel room, and you can just imagine the heart-warming scene of reunion when he came home from a hard day of shooting laundry against a sun-flooded sky.

What with her sharing his room and his meal checks, the whole tender little episode might have gone unnoticed, beyond Miami City limits. But a girl in love seems to have more *chutzpah* than the rest of us, and she had charged her ticket to Miami to the detergent account. She figured that one more location ticket wouldn't be noticed in a production budget

174

that size. But she figured without the gnome in the accounting department. He reported the extra ticket and the fat was in the fire. The lovely was fired despite the protestations of the creative director who was given his druthers. Either leave with her or stay on without her. It'll be a blow to all the romantics in the crowd to learn he opted to stay on alone. No fool, he is now one of the top bananas, creatively speaking, in the Windy City and the less said about her fate the better. Suffice it to say, her predicament today makes the little match girl look well off.

Padding location budgets, though it often goes undetected, can prove an embarrassment to all concerned. In one case, where a detergent was taking a flyer in mood commercials, the disaster that ensued merely served to drive the sudser even more deeply into his faith in slice of life commercials. Because the campaign was such a departure for a detergent, it got more than its fair share of notice and comment from the trade press.

Needless to say, the dollars involved were considerable. Just how many dollars, and how they were spent, eventually proved the downfall of one agency producer and caused a breach between the client and the agency that led to the account moving.

It was really the first time the account's production team had left the laundry rooms to go on location, and they were making the most of it. The commercials really only required showing laundry whipping airily in the bright sunshine and a brisk breeze. It probably could have been filmed right in the producer's back yard in Connecticut. But the production team sold the client on the necessity of going on location and before the campaign was shot, these creative types had strung laundry everywhere from Arizona mesas to Caribbean beaches. Mood, maybe. Empathy? Never.

The cost of all this was really mind-boggling. And the client, if not happy about it, at least was taking it like a little soldier. The account and the producer might still be at that agency except for the fact that the producer's mouth was as big as his ability to spend. On his way home from one location, he'd tucked the airline's quota of booze under his belt and was feeling somewhat expansive. After all, while all his hard-working neighbors were struggling with snow clogged driveways, he'd been spending like a drunken sailor down in Jamaica. Half the fun in such a coup, of course, is letting somebody else know about it.

Strapped in with his seat belt, I have to admit he had little choice in a confidante. He told all to the man in the next seat, elaborating glowingly about the fun he'd been having, the amount of money it was costing the client and, in a moment of ill-advised candor, he implied that the production costs were being laid on with a fairly heavy hand. It was an unfortunate admission and an even more unfortunate ear to pour it into. The man in the next seat worked for one of the big advertising trade journals and he almost parachuted out while they were in the holding pattern—he was that anxious to get the story written and published.

Needless to say, everything hit the fan the morning his paper hit the desks. The agency producer had broken the cardinal rule: Anything you take (and believe me they take plenty) has to come from the production house—not from the client. That way the agency can be in total ignorance and innocence about the whole thing. The fact that the production house has to build in these costs in their estimates—enough to cover all the kickbacks—never seems to bother anyone. After all, the bigger the production budget, the bigger the agency's commission.

Speaking of the "take," if you think agency producers settle for a case of Scotch under the Christmas tree, think again.

There's practically no limit to the largesse they'll accept—from the producer who woke up one morning to find a free Volkswagen in his driveway to the one who found a free, new garage at the end of his. The only danger the takers take, of course, is in being turned in to the Internal Revenue boys by some disgruntled fellow worker who feels he isn't getting his fair share. So rich are the pickin's, you could earn a fairly decent living just being a bounty hunter for the IRS. You can see, Virginia, why the agency producers close ranks to women. The gravy's just too rich to let the fairer sex in on it. Better they should stay writers, and stay pure.

Staying sweet and pure on location isn't all that easy. God knows you're never offered a piece of the take, but about other offers—don't ask. One of the first location jobs I ever went on was for a hair spray. The hair mavens—Revlon, Factor, et al.—already had well-established brands in the field before P&G decided to come out with theirs. To carve out their own share of the market, they were coming out with two sprays, not aimed at normal and hard-to-control hair, but rather offered as the cure for seasonal hair problems. The idea always seemed to strike a responsive chord with women when they heard about it, so we called the products Wintersett and Summersett (with no apologies to the authors involved).

Advertising being what it is, we were producing the Summersett commercial in mid-winter. So off we all went to the land of perpetual summer and continuing production, Miami.

We had shot the first commercial on a really magnificent estate on one of Miami's posher waterways—a place complete with its own dock and Mizener palace. The reason we chose it was for its charming gazebo. Things had gone as well as can be expected, considering the entire crew and cast were twelve hundred miles from their psychiatrists. There had been only minor problems: The model had forgotten her summer shoes,

177

and there'd been no rain. We solved the first problem by shooting all the long shots of her with a border of flowers between her feet and the camera. This was no problem since the place abounded in low, flowering borders. We needed a shower to prove the holding power of the hair spray, but when none showed up we pressed a sprinkler into service. It made everything look wet enough, but of course half the rain in the scene seemed to be falling up.

Of such minor problems are days on location made. Evenings are something else. While everyone was donning glad rags for din-din, I'd been catching up on the latest ax murders breathlessly reported in the Miami press. There was a knock on my door, and when the man from the production house stepped in, I braced myself for more wonderful news. Probably tomorrow's model had forgotten to bring her bathing suit. I was braced for the wrong thing, it turns out. With an incredibly few preliminary remarks, he nestled on the bed next to me and gave every indication of attempting to have his way with me.

Torn between contempt (for his features were decidedly simian) and convulsive laughter, I did my best to retain my cool. No mean trick when you're wrapped in a sheer negligee and sheets of the *Miami Herald*. Between peals of laughter, I reminded him that I was with the agency—the hiring side—in this little farce. And disengaging myself from the *Herald* and this hairy creature, I suggested he take his heavy breathing elsewhere. At dinner that night, and on other commercials we did together, the incident was totally ignored. But I never went on location with that production house again. As far as I'm concerned, location shooting doesn't *have* to make strange bedfellows.

CHAPTER XVIII

Cinéma Vérité in Cincinnati

Maybe it hasn't bothered you, but for the last few years TV commercials have made practicing Peeping Toms out of us all. As we sit in the privacy of our living rooms, the magic of the medium has taken us behind the scenes of Americans at work, at play, in some of their most intimate moments.

We've accompanied a schoolteacher on a dateless trip to Mexico only to see her turn into the Queen of the Fiesta once she's cleaned up a breath problem; we've returned from the honeymoon with the outraged groom and his terrified bride and hung around to see them kiss and make up after his shower has rid him of perspiration odor; and despite any innate distaste for ladies' bridge parties, we've shared the hostess' embarrassment when her guests start giggling behind their hands about her "housetosis."

Languishing before the set, propped up by your pillows with a sniffly cold, an afternoon of this is all very emotionally draining. The anguish of the soap opera heroines is nothing compared with the psychological stresses placed on the heroes and heroines of these mini-curtain raisers. The endless repetition of these little confrontations eventually leaves you with the thought that all of Adland is inhabited by a bunch of mindless masochists, each reliving with Freudian inevitability, her secret hangup.

There was a time, however, when you could watch endless hours of television without seeing a commercial that was any more emotionally taxing than those bitsy Busby Berkeley epics involving marching cigarettes, the Motts' singing apples, or animated characters. These used to alternate with stand-up announcers in double-breasted suits promising you the world if you would buy a used car or new storm windows from them. It was a far simpler age.

It was the age just before the movie *Marty* made the ultimate American contribution to the film form in the fifties. For once we had made a movie stripped bare (what did we know about bare in those days?) of all the Hollywood frills and polish. Here was cinéma vérité as vérité as anything that had ever come from the handheld cameras of France or Italy.

"Whaddya wanna do, Angie?"

"I donno. Wadda *you* wanna do, Marty?"

This question and its answer became the passwords to a whole new wave of film making that no one has as yet been able to stop. Americans had discovered realism, and they loved it.

The people who write commercials were quick to emulate, and the first true life vignettes began appearing on the screens. Early in the game, P&G tested one of these mini-melodramas and discovered that it scored well ahead of other kinds of commercials, including celebrity pitches. As time went on and the trend became clear that so-called slice of life commercials consistently outscored anything else, the die was cast, the rest was inevitable. The tube was sentenced to decades without end of these little atrocities.

Anyone who has ever taken a course in Psychology I, or who knows anything at all about women, can spot right away the secret of the slice's success. People, women especially, have an amazing ability to remember anything they have heard or overheard in the form of conversation. Any man who has had his wife dredge up a remark he made in passing decades ago knows the validity of this phenomenon. Give a woman a chance to eavesdrop on a conversation, and she'll be able to give you practically a word by word rerun of it later—with just a few embellishments of her own thrown in.

Those really dedicated students who go onto Psych II and learn how memory works are aware that an unfinished sentence, conversation, or story is also much more memorable than a completed one. If you've ever listened to an endless shaggy dog story only to have the teller forget the last line, you know how true this is. Last year there was an indication that someone was taking this truth to heart when Salem began running their jingle with the final "You can't take the country out of Salem" phrase cut off. I doubt if there was a person in the country who didn't mentally complete the sentence for himself. What really surprises me is that there haven't been more cliff-hangers appearing. I guess it's because every sponsor is so sure his product will bring a happy ending to your problems, he doesn't want you to miss a golden word of his carefully honed promise.

The coming of the slice of life as an art form made heroines out of a whole new breed of writer. It opened the doorway to undreamed-of success to writers who might otherwise have never made it much beyond the secretarial pool. Agency creative directors began searching for writers who could capture that elusive something called believability or realism. No longer did they yearn for inspired jingle writers or witty wordsmiths who could put together trenchant headlines. The search was on, not for people who understood advertising but for people who understood people.

181

Over and over again, in countless interviews, proof books were studied with the jaundiced eye of the critic judging a play for realistic dialogue, sincerity of motivation, dramatic flow, etc. As a result of this talent search, out of the woodworks and secretarial pools came a contingent of writers—mostly women as a matter of fact—who were held in awe as "the slice of life writers." They were cosseted, promoted, and cherished. To this day, some of the biggest corner offices are held by these ladies with a flair for the dramatic, an ear for dialogue, and no interest whatsoever in rocking the boat and trying any new advertising forms. Let those crazy, bearded kids do it, they figure. The ability to write slice of life commercials is like a trust fund, to be carefully tended and deeply appreciated. Any writer who makes the big soaps happy, makes the agency happy, too.

A friend of mine who was spinning her wheels in advertising, never making over $10,000 a year before the advent of the slice of life, is now one of the few truly secure people in the world of advertising. And the never-never land of advertising is about the only place in which she *does* feel secure. Aside from this one major talent—to tell it like it is—she is hardly the kind of writer you'd choose. She spends half her day on the phone rapping with her children's nurse and the other half complaining to her co-workers about her personal problems. And yet, between all the phone calls and the hand wringing, she manages to knock out enough of these little melodramas to keep her on her pedestal and rather splendidly compensated. Far from a chick herself, she was one of the very few survivors of one of the most brutal purges in the history of the business when B&B decided to redo their creative department to a younger, more Now image. Not only that, but right in the midst of the mass firings on every side during the business' recent sinking spell, she was able to change to an even better job at another P&G agency.

Although it was P&G who started and gave real impetus to the move toward cinéma vérité in the name of increased sales, they were soon followed by just about every other advertiser on the air. Even some cosmetic companies who should have known better tried it, until they recovered their sanity and realized no woman ever bought cosmetics for logical reasons.

Meanwhile, back in Ohio, where they love to reread and reinterpret research findings the way schoolgirls reread love letters, they were not standing still. Theirs is a dogged devotion to the pursuit of the ultimately unforgettable commercial. Somewhere along the line it was discovered that if you welded a demonstration of the product's superiority onto your little farce, you not only got better scores, but there was also the added benefit that the demonstration might convince some viewers that you had a better product. This is always nice in a competitive field. It was also discovered that if the demonstration could be worked into the situation, rather than shown in a cut-away to a lab or some such unrelated place, you scored even better. Anyhow, that's where all the legions of vignettes showing comparison mopping, scouring, and waxing started. It was the beginning of the competitive sport of getting clean. Where it will end is anybody's guess.

I had hoped they had reached their nadir when those two secretaries sprayed competitive deodorants on the elevator operator's eyeglasses, but then I caught the lady policewoman climbing into a house that was in the process of being moved, only to find some itinerant handyman washing the floors with product X (in an unmoored house stopped at a red light!). Where that feminine fuzz ever got the bucket of water to prove the superiority of Spic and Span probably puzzles that other stalwart of comparison scouring, Josephine the plumber.

It was also the relentless searching of the soaps that uncovered yet another tenet of advertising recall: It is the conversa-

183

tion, and not necessarily the emotional content of the scene that guarantees recall. That's why you see so many little housewives eyeball to eyeball across the coin-op dryer or the backyard clothesline making odious comparisons between their washes.

And because the soap companies are as universal as the dirt they are so determined to eradicate, it followed as the night the day that the slice of life commercial soon broke through the cultural and language barriers of the world and became one of our biggest exports. Another breed of international cultural heroines was born: the itinerant writer.

A friend of mine who for years had been nervously doing her thing in a cubicle at Compton got tapped for overseas duty—to bring the word of slice of life to Belgium. These little morality plays had hardly begun to roll out of her typewriter when she was recognized, revered, and rewarded with the position of creative director in the Brussels office—an absolutely unheard of position for a woman to occupy in Europe. Now back at Compton, you realize, she had been good at this game, but so had a bunch of her pals up and down the corridor. In Belgium on the other hand, and all over Europe for that matter, she was darned near unique. Slice of life commercials work equally well in Europe, and consumers empathize as much with them there as here. The stumbling block comes in trying to squeeze these little vignettes out of the local troops; European copywriters don't seem to be able to categorize people in the same warm-hearted, wonderful way Americans do. And when you've got to establish characters, a situation, and maybe half a dozen copy points in a few seconds, you've got to be able to telegraph characterization or you're running into the trained seal act.

Much as you may despise them as an art form, never underestimate the clout of the slice of life commercial, nor of the legions of ladies who can force them out of their typewriters with maddening regularity. It doesn't matter how loudly and vehemently women's lib groups rage against the demeaning simplistic view of women aired in these bathroom and laundry room dramas; as long as viewers remember and can parrot back what they've seen in those commercials, you're going to be seeing more and more of them.

And though you may not wait with bated breath to learn the outcome of these little sixty-second charades, the watching world is not made up of people like you. You can't imagine the storm of protest that was kicked up when plump, precious Alice Playten's bridegroom of the marshmallowed meatball commercial turned up across the breakfast table from that gorgeous blonde hussy in the Maxim spot! There are women out there in Videoland as upset about that as they are about any moral issues of the day.

CHAPTER XIX

Out of the Sandbox, Into the Board Room

Even before that mass of humanity, the war babies, reached the age of consent, the research boys in the back rooms of agencies started issuing rather disturbing bulletins. Advertisers are ever on the alert for changes in the consumer demographic pattern shown in their continuing nose counts, and about a decade ago a frightening figure began forming: the increasingly large number of teenagers. Manufacturers with products that could be foisted off on adolescents shifted their advertising into high gear. It was then that acne became as prevalent on TV as it is among teenagers.

The copywriter who could talk the teens' special patois was neck and neck in popularity with those gifted with a flair for slice of life writing. Even these untouchable little dramas were affected. Everything from bad breath and body odor to dandruff—the legacy of adult Americans—was quickly dropped onto the shoulders of the young. In Adland, the young were shaping up as suitable inheritors of the American dream. Just as their parents had before them, they were finding solutions to all their problems in brand name mouthwashes, deodorants, and shampoos.

It was a satisfying picture, as reassuring as it was inaccurate.

For out in the real world—beyond the sphere of influence of P&G commercial writers—all was not going as well as it was being depicted in commercials. It may, of course, be purely coincidental, or it may be another case of the cure seeking the disease, but it was also just about this time that tension headaches, frayed nerves, and sleepless nights began receiving more attention on the tube.

Just as the stalwarts of research were discovering that this great mass of young humanity was moving across the border from adolescence to young adulthood (that most glorious of all markets, the big consumer), serious students of sociology were discovering some unsettling facts about them. It wasn't long before even the least perceptive peruser of the mass media became aware that this new, Now generation was a far cry from the one that preceded it. The problems they were uptight about bore no resemblance to the things that worried their parents. In fact, they found so many things on which they disagreed with the Establishment, teenagers hardly cared how they had handled bad breath and body odor.

Any close contact with the leaders of this group quickly convinced you that current selling strategies for just about every product on the air weren't reaching this audience. It was a generation that had come home from school and been bombarded with such irresistible notions as "Feel really clean" or "Get your clothes fresh and clean as all outdoors." (This was before ecologists pointed out just how unfresh and unclean all outdoors really is.)

And when this generation, the first to have been raised with TV as its electronic baby-sitter, became old enough to vote, they turned on their parents' way of life as no generation before them ever had.

So the mindbenders of Madison Avenue were faced with a numerically enormous market which they were hopelessly unable to reach. A market that size simply cannot be ignored—no matter how unacquisitive it appeared—especially when your clients are reading about it and seeing it all around them.

It was an age of babies, boutiques and bad-mouthing the biggies. The self-anointed *wunderkind* devoted almost as much energy to knocking the big agencies as they did to patting themselves on the back. They tried to equate big with bad. Mostly, I'm convinced, because the ones who tried to make it at the big agencies—and there were some big stars who tried—really fell on their faces. Only way for them to save face was to try to put the agency down. Bates, because of its hard-sell approach, probably was on the receiving end of more of this flak than most. But it weathered all the sniping and the clients who hung in really have nothing to complain about. Those wonderful folks who gave you Panasonic have just about doubled their sales every year they've been with Bates since that well publicized creative maven was let go. It's an interesting footnote here that in the 1970 sinking spell, when other agencies were cutting back on payrolls, Bates actually was able to add to theirs. But back when the kids were taking over, who could know all that?

Historically, it was the season when the boutiquey little hot shot creative agencies broke out like a rash along Madison Avenue. The founding fathers of these were as far from the image of the agency president or board chairman as they could get. They emulated this new alienated generation in dress, mores, hairstyle and, to a degree, age. Their shtick was that they could rap with the new generation better than any stuffy old pin-striped, clean-shaven elder ever could. They made much of the fact that any client who came to them would get the personal attention and creative efforts of the agency's head honcho.

These little shops proliferated like mushrooms in a damp

season. Every time a disenchanted writer met an out-of-sorts art director for lunch, a new shop was born. The people who letter doors never had such a year. For a while, the notices of new agencies opening seemed to far exceed the number of account switches listed in the *Times* advertising column. That was one reason their clients could always deal with a founding father. There were enough founding fathers around to deal not only with every tiny client who happened along, but also to deal with lower levels of the advertising staff when a big account moved into a small shop.

Being able to deal with a president or chairman of the board when you're way down on the organizational chart acts like fine wine on a brand man. It's an enormously heady experience. This, coupled with the undeniable size of the young alienated market, made the move to small hot shops by some of the bigger accounts inevitable.

When this wave of the future appeared, two things followed just as inevitably. First, there was a proliferation of so-called service businesses (media services, research services, etc.). Second, a shock wave hit the creative departments in the big agencies, the likes of which had never before been seen.

The need for outside service companies was evident the moment the first account of any size knocked at the door of one of the new creative cult shops. When an agency is begun by a writer and an art director pooling their profit-sharing from the so-called old hat establishments, you're not likely to have much in staff beyond a buxom receptionist cum Girl Friday. An account used to the facilities of the in-depth research, media, and marketing departments of the bigger agencies may find the creative atmosphere thrilling in these new shops, but the service areas are woefully lacking.

Seeing the writing on the wall from Michael's Pub to Ratazzi's, disenchanted media men and research men began huddling over their extra-dry's and planning their own shops. It had to be one of the biggest years for new business start-ups since World War II. Shiny gold letters began popping out on doors all over the East Side.

Beads of perspiration began popping out on high-domed foreheads all over board rooms on Madison Avenue. If clients wanted the creative services of these wild-eyed, unkempt types, then they would just have to start hiring them. A sprinkling of beards, bell bottoms, and burr heads throughout their creative corridors, they reasoned, would do wonders for their creative image.

Since you can't hire without first firing, the bloodbath began. Not just elder statesmen, but most of the middle-aged members of creative departments found themselves on the streets with their proof books and their beaded bags. Collecting youths for creative departments became such a full-time game that mothers with nubile adolescent daughters or precocious prep school sons told them to avoid Madison Avenue on their way to and from school. Any writer or art director with a full set of adult molars was considered well past his (or her) prime.

But youth wasn't the only criterion for this cult. You also had to have a certain look or life style to make it into a creative department. If you were male, hair seemed to be the prime requirement: Facial, head, and chest hair became far more important indicators of your suitability than any proven ability with words or layouts. For women—I hesitate to use the word for those of such tender years—the miniest of mini skirts, hair almost the same length as the skirt and, of course, the fresh bloom of youth in evidence. Creative directors secretly vied with each other to collect the hairiest and youngest departments in town. The my-creative-department's-younger-than-yours syndrome had everybody by the throat.

190

And if you think a woman with a younger lover pursues the promise of everlasting youth, you should have seen the way some of the ladies of the Avenue behaved when this youth cult swept in. It wasn't a question of "Hate that grey?" They didn't hate it, it terrified them. As the young look took over Seventh as well as Madison Avenue, they flocked to fashions designed for girls half their age. They shortened their skirts to mid-thigh, often revealing otherwise unknown varicose veins. They tossed away their stiletto heels and began skipping to work in knee socks and Mary Janes. They showed up at work in outfits that looked like castoffs from an old Shirley Temple movie. And when creative directors had gone as far as they could without running into child labor laws or health department edicts in collecting the young and the hirsute, creative departments slipped into the most colorful phase of all.

It started in the art departments—those hot beds of bohemia—but it moved quickly into copy. Flamboyant dress became not just a style but a way of life. Nehru jackets flashed onto the scene momentarily, but were quickly discarded as too dreary and too confining. A young Jewish copywriter at D'Arcy was forced to stop wearing his dark Nehru threads when people on the street kept calling him "Father." Religious feelings aside, the word is anathema to the young, of course.

The kinkier one's clothes, the more creative one's ideas, or at least so the prevailing reasoning went. The men took to ruffled or flowered shirts and foot-wide ties. The women, not to be outdone, began wearing trousers and see-through blouses. The men then countered with suede and fringed outfits that looked more at home on the set of *Bonanza* than in an office. Forced into the area of costume, the women started pulling up to their typewriters and drawing boards in gypsy and peasant costumes, one day looking like Carmen and the next a dead ringer for Lara in *Doctor Zhivago*. People who might in saner times have been outfitted by Brooks Brothers appeared to be finding their wardrobes at Brooks Costume. Creative departments took on the look of a casting call for *Woodstock*.

In addition to sharing an eclectic taste in clothes, these new-wave tots shared certain other mannerisms. And if you wanted to hold your own in conversations or conference rooms, you had to ape them or be considered old hat and out of it. Their speech pattern was a paralyzingly repetitive one. Each sentence began with the word *like:* "Like the party last night was like a groove." Any human being who was not totally despised was invariably referred to as a "cat," and all conversations were held in a low mumble reminiscent of the scratch-and-pick Actors' Studio patois. If you were too chicken or too uptight to trip with them, you had to at least simulate their symptoms.

With all this local color on hand and on the payroll, agency heads and account men took great pride in showing it off to clients. Dark-suited clients from the Midwest or upstate would be led through the creative corridors with witty warnings from account men: "Can't take you through here at feeding time. They get quite out of hand then." And if there was a cloud of blue smoke with a slightly sweetish smell in the air, the account man would merely raise one eyebrow knowingly and shove his elbow gently into the client's ribs implying, "You see how really far out *our* creatives are." The delivery boy who used to bring the coffee in some cases was replaced by the man who brought the fix.

There was a time when you couldn't tell a creative man from an account man until he opened his mouth, but the arrival of these young gypsies changed all that. An account man in his funny little suit with his trousers matching his coat (and, my God, sometimes even a vest!) seemed more like a visitor

192

from another planet than just another department. Soon even the Harvard MBAs began to crack. Sideburns reached down toward lower lobes, shirt stripes widened perceptibly as did ties. But there was a limit on how far they could go. After all, they not only had to meet with clients, but also had to consort with them in public watering holes. The contrast between them couldn't be all *that* noticeable. And out in Suds City, no matter how much they wanted their ads to relate to the younger market, the day of the three-button, natural shoulder suit was far from dead.

The table talk when account men wined and dined clients invariably turned to tales—many of them apocryphal—of the wild comings and goings in the creative departments. I remember when I was considered eccentric just for bringing my poodle to the office. Now the most daring thing a creative person can do is to appear perfectly normal. The old joke that used to be around (that you wouldn't mind an account man in your neighborhood, but you wouldn't want your sister to marry one) was dug up and the creative man became the butt.

When Benton & Bowles moved into its new headquarters on Third Avenue, their much publicized difficulties with the phone company weren't their only problems. As in all skyscrapers, there was a certain uniformity about the size and shape of the offices as well as the fluorescent lights along the ceiling. This struck one of their new breed of writers as far too regimented. As a protest gesture, she drew her skirts about her, sat down on the floor Indian fashion, and lit a fire in the middle of her office. It was designed, she said, to take the cold impersonal chill off her little niche. It did that and a lot more. Despite the misgivings of the fire department, she is still at Benton & Bowles doing her thing by the light of a desk lamp.

Of course it's all fun and games for a client to sit around Le Madrigal or Marmiton rapping with the account man about the quaint customs of those unfettered children who took over so many creative departments when the youth cult struck. But it is something else indeed to have to deal with them in a face to face, idea to idea confrontation across the generation and culture chasm. Having once filled their creative departments with these fauna exotica, agencies were anxious to show them off. Guided tours through these creative wonderlands were mere preambles to the full dress performance of these free thinkers during presentations in conference rooms.

Clients, previously used to being presented with neatly lettered and mounted layouts and carefully executed storyboards, were shown little scraps of paper with a few scribblings that were supposed to contain the germ of breakaway advertising. Some clients, caught up in the mystique of all this undisciplined creativity being tapped for them, loved it. They felt they were there at the creation—they were an integral part of the final ad. (In many cases they actually wrote the ad during the meeting—*someone* had to.) Clients who in the past might have hesitated to completely redo an ad which looked ready to run when presented, enjoyed the easy give and take of these newly unstructured presentations.

Other clients, more adept with the stiletto than the stylus, had thoroughly enjoyed picking away, verb by verb, at ads until the beautifully executed presentation lay in a shambles around the conference room. They did not take well to this new life style. Since picayune criticism was their stock and trade, the kernel of an idea penciled onto the inside of a cigarette package gave them little to sink their teeth into. They were incapable of coming up with solutions, having spent their adult years coming up with just the problems. These clients went back to their regimented offices and fired back call reports that indicated all was not well in Cincinnati and White Plains.

Loose layouts were only part of the problem some clients had in dealing with these kids. Most of them not only looked as though they'd come straight from the sandbox to the board room, but many of them didn't seemed to have washed up on the way. You try selling a man whose livelihood depends on grabbing off one more percentage point of the soap market, ideas presented by some tot who doesn't look like she's connected with a bar of soap in a year. Try getting an OK on a shampoo commercial that's sprung from beneath one of those fuzzy hairdos that's probably harboring wildlife.

Despite the concerted rush to the fountain of youth that became a perfect mania on Madison Avenue, not every client was delirious at the thought of his multi-million-dollar ad budget being spent on what appeared to him a mere childish whim. For clients who felt that way, and among them were some of the really big spenders, the agencies were forced to keep on hand and on salary a few writers both shorter of hair and longer in tooth as well as experience. There weren't many of them, and they were never brought out and paraded around much at new business pitches, but when a campaign was needed, not a show of local color, they were the ones called on.

These are the ladies who never shortened their skirts to mid-thigh. They eschewed attempts to appear younger than springtime when actually well into summer if not early fall. They knew their business and went about it in a professional way. The tiny coterie of them who weathered the purges is now of such hardened steel that nothing short of the end of the world or the introduction of a new low sudser could ever faze them. With quiet dignity, a woman I once worked for at Benton & Bowles is sitting out this youth kick, her hearty chunk of profit-sharing and pension plan growing hourly. At this point it would probably be far cheaper for B&B to lose an account than to set this woman out to pasture. Besides, she's keeping a very large client very happy and that's a security blanket you just can't beat. You just wrap it around yourself all the way to the bank twice a month, or you pull it over your head to wait the passing or maturing of these whiz kids who require so much cleaning up after.

And if you think following one of their acts in the board room is tough, you should try traveling with this crowd who has so recently turned in its skate keys for credit cards. There is the problem of explaining them or apologizing for their bizarre behavior in areas where the Woodstock generation hasn't hit yet. Then, their very youth can make them a problem. Carol Horn, one of my writers traveling with me and some account men, was refused a drink in the Detroit airport because she was unable to prove she was twenty-one! We'd all been out on a presentation and plant tour of the Gerber plant in Fremont, Michigan. (All travel done by advertising types isn't necessarily to scenes of intrigue and romance.) Carol was wearing skirts so short that every time she leaned over a vat of strained peas, I was sure the plant manager would suffer a cardiac arrest. It was also her first trip away from home, unaccompanied by her parents, and she excused herself almost hourly from meetings and meals to phone her mother.

I knew an account man once who refused to travel out to a certain garden spot in the Midwest with one of my writers because he said taking her to the Newark airport made him feel as though he were violating the Mann Act. In an age where anything goes between consenting adults, it wasn't really as hard to get the consent of some of these younger ladies of the Avenue as it was to get proof that they were adults!

CHAPTER XX

Shortsighted Memos and Blind Carbons

There was a time when the funniest reading around was the inter-office memos that piled up in the in boxes along Madison Avenue. But ever since the appearance of Helen Gurley Brown's bosom dispatch to her staff at *Cosmopolitan* a while back, advertising has had to take second place to publishing in the memo derby. For any of you who were living under rocks or not subscribing to *Women's Wear Daily* at the time, the memo in question was one circulated to the *Cosmopolitan* staff (one would assume only to the female staff members), asking them to detail how they preferred to have their breasts manipulated in the course of lovemaking.

There is little on record as to what the general reaction of the staff was to this memo—except for one young lady who evidently felt that it was significant enough to warrant sending it on to a friend at *Women's Wear Daily*. They were quick to recognize its influence on the life style of the day and gave it prominent space in their pages. It has become the classic memo of the sixties. But the seventies topped it with Cosmo's survey on multiple orgasms. On Madison Avenue, though the memos may have lacked some of the color of the ones in publishing, they still had a great deal to recommend them as light reading.

Like all great humor, most of it was unplanned and unintentional. Account executives who felt they were really a lot more creative than the creative types realized, took to the memo format to prove their point. One of my most favorite memos came not to me but to a friend in another copy group. It was from an account executive and it accompanied a work order for some new campaign ideas on his account. It ended with a line that even in the never-never land of memo writing must be a near classic; it urged his entire copy group to "put every ounce of inertia behind it." Needless to say they were more than happy to oblige. This same friend also received a rather lengthy dissertation from one of her clients which included the request that his product "always be surrounded with an aurora of elegance."

But it isn't only the account man and the client who are apt to come a cropper in a memo. Reputations and men were made and broken by memos, and the creative types are not immune. I once worked for a man who had worked his way literally down Madison Avenue from a really good job in a really good shop to a spot on the beach in front of a really fading one, strictly on the strength of his memos. He just couldn't restrain his enthusiasm for the memo as both a defensive and offensive weapon.

Whenever he returned from a meeting where he felt he or one of his ideas had been put down unreasonably, he would rush to his SCM, throw himself on the keys, and pour out his anguish and anger and whatever else hadn't settled well with him that day. His memos were models of wordy vituperation. Though they were cleverly conceived, they were brought forth in more heat than light. They expressed all the pent-up feelings he was either too shy or too incoherent to express verbally at meetings. He'd have been far better off telling people to go to hell than putting it in a memo. The spoken word may never be called back, but at least it isn't down there in black and white to haunt you the way a memo is.

The memo has strange ways of reappearing, and once out of your out box it has a life of its own, quite disconnected from anything you may have intended for it. My former copy supervisor, for instance, used the memo to clear the air and get a few feelings and bon mots out of his system. Had he the sense of a child of eight, he would have poured out his feelings and furies in the memo and then torn it carefully into shreds. But he never did; his collected memos when bound would probably have filled a five-foot shelf in your library. They really should have been required reading for anybody tempted by the memo as a form of expression. Better graffiti on latrine walls, or poems submitted to the *Times*.

When I last ran into my memo-writing, former supervisor, he was one-quarter of the way through a novel and already had close to 200,000 words written. Madison Avenue may have lost him, but he still has his enthusiasm for the written word. And his tendency to run off at the keys whenever he sits down at a typewriter now appears to be incurable.

Despite what you may read in learned works about working your way up the executive ladder by memo writing (and I must admit, it has worked wonders in many cases), there are more rungs on the corporate ladder made slick and slippery by ill-advised or shortsighted memos than can be recounted. Much more fun, and a far less deadly medium, is the letter.

Since agencies never sign their ads, whenever a campaign or a single ad, or even a line or word, rubs the public the wrong way, it's the client who hears about it first. The more outraged the letter, the faster it gets back to the writer at the agency. All complimentary letters—and don't scoff at the notion, there really are some—stay firmly in the client's hands and files. In fact, until I actually went to work on the client's side of the desk, I'd never even seen any of these complimentary ones. But I've seen more than enough of the others.

You can imagine the amount of hand wringing that went into the decision to run a line like "For the first time in your life, feel really clean." The key word here, of course, is feel. Nobody wanted to imply that you've never been really clean. But with this new bath product that didn't leave behind any sticky old soap film, you'd really *feel* the difference. Sure, feel was the key word, but a lot of the people who saw and heard the advertising hadn't been in on all those handwringing sessions back at the agency—so the outraged letters began pouring in. "What do you mean, for the *first* time in my life, you think I'm a slob or something?" was the general drift.

When you've a quarter of a million female representatives selling your products, you're just bound to have some pretty special customer relations. That explains both the volume and some of the volubility of mail the company I'm now with receives: Maybe nudity has spread from the skin flicks and the art houses to the neighborhood movie in your town, but not where our customers live. They are so down on nudity they even resent an ad showing a girl undressed in a tub, despite the fact the wildly foaming bubble bath covers her up to her armpits. Makes you kind of wonder if there are people out there somewhere bathing fully dressed. We heard from them, too, when we showed a nude (mind you all anatomical indications of her sex were hidden) applying a body lotion. How you can apply that fully clothed is another puzzler.

But if the keepers of the moral tone are ever at their pens, the newly active women's lib groups are not far behind. Not only do we get the usual form letters (with only the name of the company written in by hand) threatening us with a boycott, but we sometimes hear from the really far out. One "mother of three little girls" (poor darlings) wrote us in high dudgeon, accusing us of making sex symbols of little girls in our ads. She based her charge on the fact that we have a line of little girls' products—bubble bath and shampoo—packaged in little dolls and toy shaped little soaps! If that's her idea of a sex symbol, it's a wonder her three daughters ever arrived. Every one of these letters is answered with great care, not by some whirring computer but by some charming ladies of good heart and the patience of saints.

You really never know what kind of consumer reaction you're going to uncork when you write a line. Certainly no one at Wells, Rich, Greene ever thought they'd unleash the librarians with a little throwaway line in one of their ads for Javelin. To prove what a swinging car they were peddling, they used the line, "We may lose a few librarians for customers, but. . . ." You bet your sweet bumper they lost the librarians —not with the car but with the ad. All those swinging librarians out there grabbed the pencils they usually have stuck in their buns and let American Motors know in no uncertain terms what they thought of a company that downgrades an entire profession by fostering inaccurate stereotypes about it.

But it's in memos, not letters, where the real game is played. My former copy supervisor made one of the mistakes people who don't understand the purposes of memos make. He put into writing things that should never have been put down in black and white, to say nothing of in triplicate carbons. Another mistake the newcomer to Madison Avenue is apt to make is to consider a memo merely a method of communicating information. Nothing could be further from the truth; the actual transfer of information is the least important purpose of any memo.

At one agency where I worked, they had a peculiar kind of

201

memo called a Call Report that was written up and sent out after any contact with a client, and after any agency meeting in which anything more was discussed than the weather and where to have lunch. The avowed purpose of these call reports, and they rained like a deluge on some of the accounts, was to keep people informed on what was going on with the account. All the people who were actually at any meeting were listed, and in the case of a really big account, the agency's head honchos were also to receive the memo. Copies, too, were sent to the client so that he'd know just how many people at the agency really cared about his account. Listed in blind carbons would usually be the lackey on the account whose job it was to act on the information contained therein. One of the status symbols at that agency (beside the title on the door) was having your name listed right up there under the big guys rather than on a blind carbon. Who you actually listed on your memos to receive copies, of course, was an indication of where you felt you belonged in the agency pecking order. So there was a lot of shuffling and rethinking of names before any memo went out from someone who was the least bit insecure.

Once you'd decided who should be listed to receive the memo and who should be unlisted but still receive it, the really creative work began. If practically no progress was made at a meeting, you could hardly write that in your call report. You had to find ways to make a wasted two and a half hours look like great strides forward had been made by everyone who attended. As well as serving as progress reports, call reports—just as any run of the mill memo—were often used for the subtle put down. It had to be subtly done or you got known as a sore head and not a team player—like the man who is now working on his 800,000 word novel. Because of the imaginative reportage of the events in them and their various side uses, the reading of an inter-office memo became a highly developed skill.

An even more highly developed skill was one developed by Barbara Eckman, a witty and wonderful copywriter whose job never was enough of a challenge for her imagination. Whenever a particularly pedantic memo would come across her desk, she would write between its lines, making it a joy to read and eliminating the strain of reading between the lines for those of us who were not good at the game. One of her best efforts follows, with the original memo in capitals and Barbara's helpful thoughts in lower case. All owners of this book can consider themselves listed as receiving it, all borrowers as blind-copied.

TO THE STAFF:

BECAUSE WE SPEND AN AVERAGE OF SEVEN HOURS A DAY AT D'ARCY, MANY OF US THINK of this agency as some kind of living hell. An occasional kook thinks OF THIS OFFICE AS A SORT OF SECOND HOME. BUT THERE *IS* A DIFFERENCE. HERE WE have air conditioning. There is none in hell; damn little at home. Here we ARE UNDER CONSTANT INSPECTION BY VISITORS, MANY OF WHOM ARE CLIENTS—AS WELL as media representatives, job seekers, models, actors, who'll steal our money as fast AS MEMBERS OF OUR OWN STAFF.

IN THIS BUSINESS, WHERE IMAGES ARE SO IMPORTANT, LET'S LOOK AT OURSELVES. Everybody get a mirror. An ironing board will be put in the reception rooms. SUPPOSE *YOU* WERE AN OUTSIDER VISITING YOUR DEPARTMENT FOR THE FIRST TIME. Are those pants creases neat? Those fingernails clean? Those noses powdered? WHAT WOULD BE *YOUR* IMPRESSION OF D'ARCY? I ask you.

FORTUNATELY WE CAN DO A LOT TO IMPROVE OUR OWN IMAGE. HERE ARE SOME SUGGESTIONS. Everybody get a D'Arcy uniform. This will give us a uniform look. Shower daily. YOU MAY HAVE OTHERS.

1. GET RID OF MATERIAL THAT IS CLUTTERING YOUR DESK OR THE EMPTY DESKS in the empty offices that surround you. Don't keep that dirty Kleenex AROUND YOU. IF IT SHOULD BE FILED, PUT IT INTO THE CABINET WHERE IT will spread germs only to the adjacent material. Be sure to file it where it BELONGS. IF IT IS ONLY TAKING UP SPACE, PUT IT IN THE WASTE BASKET.

2. TAKE YOUR COFFEE BREAKS AS INCONSPIC-UOUSLY AS POSSIBLE. AFTER ALL, Schrafft's coffee can poison you. If your boss asks you to get some, tell him THIS IS A BUSINESS OFFICE, NOT A CAFETE-RIA—AND GET RID OF YOUR boss as fast as you possibly can—maybe you could throw him out with the COF-FEE CUPS AS SOON AS YOUR COFFEE BREAK IS OVER.

3. DON'T BE A DRIFTER. HANGING AROUND OTHER PEOPLE'S DESKS HINDERS THEIR bill-paying, personal letters and phone calls. It may lead you into extra WORK AND KEEPS YOU AWAY FROM YOUR OWN PHONES. IT ALSO GIVES EVERYONE the idea that we are a friendly, nice bunch of people instead of THE IMPRESSION THAT YOU'RE NOT BUSY.

4. UNNECESSARY NOISE IS DISTRACTING TO YOUR FELLOW WORKERS, AS WELL AS misleading people into thinking something is going on here. Don't

204

speak TO VISITORS. IT'S NOT POSSIBLE TO ELIM-
INATE THE RINGING OF PHONES OR anything like
that, but try to keep them off the hook. Do eliminate THE
CLACKING OF TYPEWRITERS, BUT YOU CAN
KEEP YOUR VOICE LOW, once you don't have to con-
tend with these other sounds.

WE ALL WANT D'ARCY TO SHINE BY COMPARISON
WITH OTHER AGENCIES. LET'S SEE WHAT exception-
ally good creative work will do, because God knows there is little that GOOD HOUSEKEEPING CAN CONTRIBUTE.

CHAPTER XXI

As Long as You Spell My Name Right

A PR maven I once shared an apartment with taught me the only thing I know about publicity: "Never care what they say about you as long as they spell your name right." Since her name's Electra Bilmazes, even that small stipulation was hard to meet. But in a trade press that can kill a campaign, a career, or an agency with a planted or inadvertent rumor, that rule of thumb doesn't work.

Since everyone outside of contemplative monastic orders can hardly avoid radio, television, newspapers, magazines, or billboards, just about everyone is fully aware of what the advertising agencies have been doing recently. This puts the ad trade press in a bit of a quandary. Unlike other trade presses, they've really no need to reveal what the competing agencies are doing. For a business that thrives on rumors, the ad trade press must know and reveal what the agencies are *about* to do. It puts them into the unenviable position of being keyhole watchers, eavesdroppers, gossip mongers, and, to a degree, prophets. They tend to be considered by some advertising practitioners with no more honor than a prophet in his own country.

In a business where an agency's very life can depend on the

whim or will of one or two powerful clients, rumors about a client's discontent or dissatisfaction can easily kick off the musical chairs game that is played whenever a big piece of business changes agencies. This doesn't make the press less apt to run rumors; it just adds excitement to the game.

In New York today, far and away more people read the advertising news column of *The New York Times* than any other source of news about Madison Avenue. It not only carries the clout of the prestigious *Times*, it just happens to be the only game in town when it comes to daily reporting on the business. (Despite its name, *Ad Daily* is a twice weekly item appearing on Wednesdays and Fridays.)

The *Times* advertising column, under Mr. Phil Dougherty's guidance, never prints rumors. Just the facts. And while Mr. Dougherty evidently attends his share of press lunches, breakfasts, and campaign previews, hemmed in as he is by the paper's refusal to play the rumor game, the column often reads a bit like a collection of PR releases. Forced to stay within the perimeter of fact, it becomes almost a Madison Avenue version of *That Was The Day That Was*. And in a business so atune to rumors, where nothing is deader than today's news, Mr. D. must have his hands full just keeping the crowd awake.

If there is only one source of daily news about the Avenue in New York, there is certainly no shortage of less frequent, more colorful coverage. Everything from *Ad Age* and *ANNY* (*Advertising News of New York*) to *Ad Daily* and *The Gallagher Report*. In something of a class by itself is New York based *Madison Avenue*, a slick monthly that after twelve years of publishing fell on hard times and suspended publishing for a few months. But with a recent financial shot in the arm, it was due back in the spring. In a trade press not long on looks, it was not only the best looking by far, but could also compete with any of the consumer slicks on the stands. As a monthly, it could hardly carry much in the way of news. So it made a strength of what could have been a weakness and concentrated on personality, campaign, client, and agency profiles. The in-depth journalistic report became *Madison Avenue*'s thing. It was a smart looking periodical, sort of the coffee table magazine of the ad trade.

Unlike the trade press for other industries which, with the exception of *Women's Wear Daily*, is a big yawn for those not in that particular trade, the advertising press with its diversity seems to have a little something for everyone. While they all report news of the same industry, their viewpoint and depth vary considerably.

Despite the fact that New York is the center of the advertising world, the big daddy of the ad trade press just happens to be Chicago-based *Advertising Age*. It is the bible of the industry, and its various special annual editions are often kept as reference works. No item of news seems to be too small to find its way into *Ad Age*'s pages. They've room in their big 15" by 11" format (sometimes running to over one hundred pages per issue) for everything from major account shifts to the promotion of minor media men in Dayton. Their eye is truly on the sparrow, and no sparrow ruffles its plumage without full coverage in *Ad Age*. If your mother likes to see your name in print and you are even remotely connected with advertising, send her a subscription to *Ad Age* for Christmas. It couldn't hurt, and it could keep her busy looking for your name. It is a trenchant comment on the proliferation of titles in the ad business to note that, even in a publication the size of *Ad Age*, there is room only to list those fortunates named VPs since the preceding Monday's issue. Nor is any space wasted on the kind of human interest that goes into the publicity releases about these mass elevations. In a weekly column titled "Agency People," is

208

a paragraph headed "Elected VPs." You get your name and your agency's name, and that's it.

Ad Age reports new campaigns that break and usually has a sprinkling of pictures of ad people disporting themselves at conventions, meetings, and luncheons, or crowning the triumphant new Miss Independent Typesetters of Milwaukee. They are given to quoting entire speeches of members of the advertising profession. And except for the drinking you might miss out on, there is really no need to attend any convention *Ad Age* is covering, their reportage is that complete. The weight of their pre-Christmas and annual review issues makes it a paper you can't send a small boy to pick up.

If you risk a hernia picking up a copy of *Ad Age*, you run the risk of a cardiac arrest flipping through the four to six baby blue pages of *The Gallagher Report*. They may be apocryphal, but there are stories of anxious ad men picking up *Gallagher* each week to see if they've been fired. And if you can depend on *Ad Age* to give you the details of what's happened, you can just as surely depend on *Gallagher* to give you a pretty good idea of what's going to happen. *The Report* has an eerie ability to foreshadow that would do a Gothic novelist proud. It's no crystal ball that does it, but rather a unique open ear to the rumblings along the Avenue, and some of the best placed sources in the business. At one of the agencies where I worked, you wouldn't dare be caught with a *Gallagher Report* on your desk or you'd be suspect. The chairman of the board was so paranoid about rooting out a suspected "informer" that he fired a clutch of men closest to him. What's really funny is that the chairman is now long gone and the source is still there.

For someone with as avid an interest in what's going on near the various seats of power along the Avenue and as short an attention span as I have, *The Gallagher Report* has to be the fastest reading in town. Just how far ahead you can keep by following *Gallagher* is shown in the different dates and articles covering just one of the autumn rites along the Avenue.

During the month of November, 1970, everybody was watching and reporting on the infighting that preceded the disappearance of the D'Arcy agency as an entity in its merger with MacManus, John & Adams. (*Gallagher* readers had actually been watching since October.) In a twelve hundred word, front page story on November 9th, *Advertising Age*, under the headline, "Lewis seeks to enjoin D'Arcy; Asks $15,000,000," detailed both Lewis' suit and the agency's counterclaims. They charged him with among other things, "rank disobedience, misfeance and malfeance," and cited the loss of $27,000,000 in billings since his takeover. The November 10th *Gallagher Report* announced that Lewis had dropped the suit and it was being settled out of court for $1.3 million. (*Gallagher* in its lead article on October 14th had predicted the legal action taken by Lewis.) On November 16th, both *Ad Age* and the *Times* ad column announced the out of court settlement.

A lot of people who wouldn't miss a word in *The Gallagher Report* complain about it, claiming it causes a lot of unnecessary fear along our street. But as my favorite President was wont to say, "If you can't stand the heat, get out of the kitchen."

Appearing on the same baby blue paper and sharing the same small four page format is the twice weekly *Ad Daily*. This six-year-old entry looks a bit like a knock-off of the nineteen-year-old *Gallagher Report*. It, too, has sources all around the town. And like *The Gallagher Report*, it is sold by subscription only and never takes advertising. You don't really need much financial help when your subscriptions go for $28 and $36 a year.

Both *Ad Age* and *ANNY* carry paid classified ads including help and position wanted ones. But Ed Buxton, the editor and publisher of *Ad Daily*, runs what amounts to a job clearing house right in the pages of his newsletter, no fees, please. He has thus endeared himself to a large portion of the Adland population. If it's true you can hear about losing your job in *Gallagher*, isn't it heartwarming to know you can find another one in *Ad Daily*? It's only fair.

CHAPTER XXII

The Migratory Birds

He's a silver-maned, Dutch uncle type who happens to be the head of all creation at one of the bigger agencies in London, and he has his own theory about the migratory birds. He thinks the ladies of Madison Avenue who come to London do so for one of three reasons: because of a man in the United States, because of a man in London, or because of no man at all.

To prove his point, he described the circumstances surrounding the migration of several birds he knew. A delightful girl who had worked for him in the states found herself deeply in love with a man tied securely to his mother's apron strings. By putting an ocean between them, she hoped to force a little distance between him and his mother. She stayed in London for a year, during which time he'd flown over several times, swearing his undying love and promising to mend his ways. He never did pop the essential question, but she hated to see him wasting his money on all those airline tickets. So she's back in the states now working at a New York agency and living in a *ménage à trois*—which, if it is not totally satisfying to those concerned, is at least saving him all that airfare.

Then there's the J. Walter Thompson writer who found love

212

and happiness while in London on location and just stayed on after the rest of the crew packed up their cameras and went home. She was a crackerjack writer who had no trouble finding a job. In fact she had several offers almost immediately, and has settled happily into an American-based agency.

My friend also told me about a girl who was a free-fall nut. She found herself involved with a man she didn't feel was quite right for her and decided to end it all by putting an ocean between them. She's been there almost two years and he's been over three times. (These girls must be the darlings of the airlines.)

Then there was the one our Dutch uncle calls the "older woman" (she's thirty so that should give you some notion of just how far this youthquake nonsense has spread). She loves to travel and by making London her home base, she's put herself some three thousand miles closer to just about any place she wants to go.

I'm not so sure he's right about there only being three reasons for the migration. Many women are married and come when their husbands are transferred; others just want to try living abroad; and, of course, there are the ones who just weren't making it in New York and rather than start the downhill circuit, they opt for London where at least they can cover their motives. Besides, in London, there's an undeniable respect for American advertising practitioners—no matter how grudging it may be. And they need never know that you can't get past the receptionists on Madison Avenue.

Some of the girls I know just wanted to be a part of the swinging London scene. One thing's certain: No girl ever went to London to seriously further her career. But when you're twenty-two as Mary is and you have long blonde hair down to your waist, big hazel eyes, and a desire to see the world, the fact that you're not doing your career much good hardly mat-

213

ters at all. It's almost post-graduate study for the girls like her. She graduated from Mount Holyoke, worked a few months in New York for an English agency (how's that for turning the tables?), and then came over to London where she continued to work for the same agency for several months before switching to the London office of an American shop. She finds the living costs high and the living arrangements a bit odd.

For a short time she shared a flat with two other girls and two men. This mixed sex, flatmate thing is really quite widespread in London. She also found Englishmen quite reserved and difficult to get to know. Expatriate she may be, but she resents certain English attitudes toward Americans—especially the fact that they make fun of Americans' openness and friendliness. She is aware in work, however, that a lot of their teasing is tinged with resentment and a hard-to-admit respect for American know-how. She hopes some day to move on to Paris or Rome although the language barrier may be a bit of a stumbling block there.

Speaking of the language barrier, one English art director I spoke to about working with American women said he found them easy enough to work with until they hit what he called phase two. According to him, all Americans go through three phases if they stay in England long enough. During the first phase they speak in the idioms and slang known only to fellow Americans and assume the English understand everything they're saying. In phase two they assume the English they're talking to know nothing of what they're saying. As Paul said, you often hear explanations of words like carport and carpet. Dealing with Americans in phase two, Paul claims, you find yourself using the phrase, "Yes, yes I understand," like some broken record. Phase three, if one has the patience to get to it, finds the American with a rough idea of the language differences as well as the scope of their similarities.

214

Another sweet young thing Madison Avenue lost to London was an art trainee in New York when she met and fell for a copy cub in the same agency. They pooled their resources and went to London. She found work right away, but he looked for several weeks before finding a spot in an English agency. Now they're saving their pennies, which are few since they both took sizable salary cuts when they made the move, to buy an antique Rolls Royce. They plan to tour Europe in it someday and then take it back to the States with them. The money they get for the Rolls here will be a little nest egg with which they hope to start out all over again. "Out West someplace. Not in advertising. Not in New York, definitely."

Both Mary and this sweet young thing agree on a lot of things about London, and neither is ready or willing to go back to New York now or in the foreseeable future. They both found living costs higher and living conditions a lot bleaker than they'd expected. They both miss central heating, even though one of them had only been there from August to November when I spoke to her. They find the English harder to get to know than Americans, and English agencies far less efficient than American ones—even those that are branches of American shops. They are both amazed at the amount of sex they find in advertising in Europe, but especially in England.

I found it a bit of a surprise myself to find sex screaming out at you from every billboard in dignified, diffident England. I understand extreme close-ups of different portions of the body seem to follow each other in popularity. A few months ago, it was crotch shots; now it is legs and thighs that seem to be in. But the really amazing part of it all is not just the nudity and innuendo of the advertising, but the wide variety of products and services which they feel warrant the use of sex. It's no challenge, of course, to get sex into the posters for perfume, lingerie, cosmetics and so forth. But to get it into the advertising for a little chain of shoemakers—that's a challenge. If you're stumped on that one, picture this season's classic shot: the inside of the leg from the toe to the upper thigh, and a girl's hand slipping her shoe off. Top it with the headline: "More girls take theirs off for us." You see how simple it is once you put your mind to it.

The Sensuous Woman was being serialized in one of the city's dailies when I was last in London. You can imagine the writhing and thrashing about among the satin sheets that appeared in the telly plugs for that newspaper. Kind of a folksy footnote was added to this display of ecstasy when the announcer, a sincere, buttoned-up type, appeared on the screen, walked to the edge of the bed, sat down, faced the camera, and without paying any heed whatsoever to the lovely writhing on the bed proceeded to pitch for the series, book in hand. God, they don't make self-control like that in this country!

The number of morning-after scenes on posters and on the telly is mind boggling, but they seem always to fit one pattern. She's in the foreground, stretching and yawning or looking misty and satisfied depending on the art director's whim; he's in the rumpled bed in the background, sleeping soundly; there is the required disarray of hastily removed clothing lying about. And copy, brief but to the point: "When you really mean it!" This popular scene is used to sell everything from mouthwash to mattresses.

Cheek by jowl with all this blatant sexuality, on the billboards in every underground station, you'll find equally enticing ones offering the services of friendly local stations in practically every neighborhood where pregnancy tests are "quick, convenient, discreet." One would hope so under the circumstances.

But despite, or maybe because of, their rather Danish acceptance of sex, advertising agencies in London have much to recommend them to the American girl looking for a new way of life, a change of pace, or just a nice place to visit.

London is a truly magnificent city with a skyline and a way of life left over from far more gracious eras. It's the kind of city any girl who grew up on Jane Austen and Gothic novels dreams of living in. And for the past few years, on top of all the traditional paraphernalia, panoply, pomp, and circumstance has been added a swinging society, an elite of the young, the gifted, the creative. It's an almost irresistible combination of lures. And the fact that so many American ladies of the Avenue have migrated there is not as surprising as the fact that even more haven't.

Travel writers and romantic novelists used to categorize Paris as a woman's city and London as a man's. They couldn't be further from the truth. Of course London was designed for the comfort and ease of English gentlemen, and it's one of the cities in the world where the women's lib groups will undoubtedly find the stickiest going, but London is becoming to a woman in a way which Paris could never be. Paris vies with a woman for attention and admiration; London doesn't: London provides the smartest of all backgrounds for her. Like a handsome man, it's the most flattering accessory a girl can have. It's an easy town for a girl to shine in, especially the girls who are going over now. They've got that wide-eyed, enthusiastic, young look of expectancy. And they're over there not to be convinced, but to love it. It's all part of the excitement of being a new-girl-in-town. On top of that, add the recognition that these girls are the real pros from the advertising capital of the world, and they've a know-how and a professional patina no London girl—or man—has.

They also have—and this is not universally admired—a stronger drive and more ambition than their London sisters. It's expressed in lots of different ways by those maddeningly reticent Englishmen, of course, but the meaning is all the same. "English women don't seem to take their work as seriously," they're apt to say with a smug smile barely concealed.

At a small dinner party in Kensington, I had forced the conversation—a desultory recap of an even more desultory cricket match—onto the subject of women in business, hoping slyly to draw them out on the subject of American women in London agencies. My visit was almost over, and a combination of English reserve and reticence had made it next to impossible for me to get any statement of fact or feeling on the subject. This might possibly be due to the fact that my hostess was an American girl who had made the trip across the pond about four years ago and was now practically passing as English. Whether they really felt that way, or whether it was just an inborn tact, every one of them preceded each statement on the subject with the words, "Of course, Nancy's quite atypical." This time I thought I might come in the back way on the subject by bringing up the women's lib movement and some of its ideas about equal pay for equal work. Had I dunked my feet into my fingerbowl, I wouldn't have gotten a bigger reaction. The man from the City on my right cleared his throat importantly and proclaimed that he never could and never would—no matter how badly off he might be—work with or for a woman. "Of course, thank heavens, it could never happen in the City," he added gratefully. "A woman's place is in the home." He sure could turn a pretty phrase when pressed.

His wife, a slightly plumpish blonde with that Dresden doll complexion that only grows in damp climates where there is no central heating, gazed at him with adoration and never said a word. You can imagine my surprise when I learned over port and hardtack that she was one of the most successful commercial film producers in England. I'm not so sure American women have more ambition; I just think maybe they don't

218

cover it up as well as English women do. I wonder what would happen if it were the truly ambitious ladies of the Avenue who were migrating instead of those more interested in a change of climate than an improvement in rank.

If there is this lack of ambition among English women, I'm sure it has been trained into them by the British educational system. The emphasis on home and hearth in their upbringing is enough to curl the hair of your neighborhood woman's liberationist. To English girls, an office is just a place to spend the time waiting for Mr. Right to provide a replica of the secure little nest from which they sprang.

An American creative director, who is in London working out his contract with an agency on Third Avenue known for its revolving door personnel policy, puts the blame for the lack of copywriters on the British educational system. According to this temporary transplant, education for the great majority of English children stops at sixteen. Beyond that there are many so-called technical schools but no real art school; there simply isn't the mass of liberal arts graduates from which most American copywriters come. That's just one of the reasons the ladies of the Avenue have been finding the red carpet out for them in London for so long.

As soon as he mentioned the lack of liberal arts graduates, I immediately thought of all those Oxford and Cambridge types being graduated each year. It wasn't until much later I discovered that the graduates of those two venerable institutions don't seem to feel advertising is a proper calling. They go into science, law, church, military, or the City, but so far, there is still a stigma on the profession of huckstering that Americans have pretty well outgrown.

Not knowing this, I expected the halls of advertising there to be chockablock full of chinless wonders, all sporting the old school tie the way the halls of Madison Avenue used to groan under the weight of Ivy League types. That's so far from the case that one rather extensive office of an American agency can boast only one Eton old boy. They fell heir to this treasure only because he couldn't make it into either Oxford or Cambridge. The chances of an Eton graduate being turned down by one of those schools is about as likely as Alabama State Teachers College turning down a Choate graduate in this country.

But enough of the old boys and back to the girls. Whether they come, as my friend said, because they can't get the man or the job they want in New York, they all discover certain hard facts of life when they get there. The first one is usually financial. Whatever you've heard about things being cheaper in London—to make up for the insane difference in salary levels—you can forget. Rents are maybe 5 to 10 per cent less. But that's usually on a flat with no central heating and plumbing that was installed at about the same time Victoria was. So baroque and erratic is it, that you find yourself feeling a secret little thrill of pleasure every time you manage to successfully flush the loo.

Nor can you always depend on a compatriot for proper sympathy. A friend of mine, living on an English salary, asked her American creative head for a raise and was told not to worry about putting anything aside for her old age as the government's national health and welfare program would take care of her. Fortunately she has since found employment with another American-connected agency with a less barbaric attitude about young ladies who are trying to support themselves with their typewriters.

The notion that you can live on a lot less in London, of course, is widely held by almost everyone who has never tried it. It is an ugly rumor spread about by bargain-hunting creative directors who are invariably over there on fat American salaries which buy a lot more than they did in New York. One creative director I interviewed who was pushing this erroneous idea, especially among his employees, argued that theater tickets and public transportation are a lot cheaper in London than in New York. So assuming you plan to spend your time shuttling back and forth on the underground between performances, and eschewing a flat and three squares a day, you might enjoy making do on an English salary. Actually, before the interview was over, he offered the following piece of advice to young girls planning to come to London to work: Make your job arrangements in New York and nail down an American salary before packing.

A friend of mine claims to be the very first lady of the Avenue to make the move to England. First or not, she remains a model all might well follow. She was sent to London by the New York agency for which she worked, all expenses paid. And they were considerable since she took her husband and small son as well as a houseful of furniture. She also took with her a rather handsome salary—even by American standards. This she arranged to have paid to her in an intricate way using English money, American money, and a very understanding little banker in Switzerland. With all this she was paid just a few shillings less than the Queen and considerably more than the agency's managing director. He's the head honcho for all you who don't speak the Queen's English.

Procter and Gamble up in Newcastle were flattered to death to have her services, and of course the agency did a good bit of parading her around proudly. It was really a super experience for her until other Americans broke ranks and agreed to come play the same game for a lot lower stakes. Turns out, you see, that London wasn't the high risk, hardship area they thought

221

it was back in New York where anyone who lived beyond Greenwich got a travel allowance and a lot of loving care. It only lasted a few years, but it was a gas while it did.

Another friend of mine might well be an inspiration to us all. She had started down the dreary road that leads from New York to Chicago to wherever when she moved to London. There she was one of the early birds who caught more than worms. She had her choice of jobs, and in fact became so jaded with it all that she had soon given up full-time work entirely, preferring to free-lance for several agencies at once. They became a bit cross about it all when they discovered the promiscuity of her creativity, but by then she had put together a fat little bundle, part of which she used to purchase and furnish a duplex in Belgravia. This she rents out for over a hundred pounds a week which is quite a bit more than most copywriters over there make. And whenever she has a sinking spell, she takes herself off to one of the chic-er watering spots and lives off her rent money. Work is something she reads about—with considerable distaste, I might add.

Now the pickings are a lot slimmer. A girl has to do more than just bat her big blue eyes in the direction of London to land a job there. And the job she lands, unless it has been arranged in this country, makes for pretty grim living conditions. But it's great fun for the young, and it's even greater fun for the unemployed Americans whose number now seems to be legion.

One reason things have tightened up there is the great number of Americans who came swarming over, once the word was out about the red carpet treatment they'd receive. And the moment England gave up its banker's grey image for the flashier one of Carnaby Street, the young flocked over. As a result of this invasion, or just in the natural course of events, London advertising is now light-years ahead of what it was even six years ago.

According to an American creative director over there who had best remain anonymous, they've made enormous strides in the last few years. In his opinion, their quality is now up to American standards, although they are not as innovative. He's the same man who feels that Britain is making a mistake trying to keep pace with the industrial giants like the USA and Germany, and should content themselves with being a service nation. They make the world's best butlers and tour guides he assured me. Britain—a nation of butlers and tour guides?! That's why he'd best remain anonymous.

He represents an interesting kind of transplant himself. A wave of the past, as a matter of fact, that washed up on Britain's shores a few years ago—a bit after the invasion by the ladies. He's one of the legion of men working out their contracts overseas and out of sight. In his case, out of sight does not mean he is in any way out of trouble.

When you've been in the business as long as these men have, you realize that it is not the sweet talk, the corner office, the unlimited expense account, or even the big dollars that matter most; it's the contract. And back in the good old days, before Mr. Nixon decided that having half your friends on the street was an acceptable level of unemployment, these contracts were fairly easy to come by. Now they're literally worth their weight in gold.

Before American agencies discovered England as a good place to stow their skeletons, anyone who had fallen from grace before his contract ran out could be a severe embarrassment to a company. Either he had to be bought off outright, which he seldom was since that was just putting free money into the pocket of someone the agency was really down on, or

223

else he was made to sweat it out, coming into the office regularly with little or nothing to do. His clout was either taken away in one swift stroke or gradually eroded away, memo by memo.

But a few years ago when the American agencies started acquiring or setting up foreign branches, they discovered what super places they were for old soldiers who refused to die or fade away with any discretion. It was like finding a place in the country for mad, old aunt Martha. And so the executive exodus began. Now you'll find them all over Europe, working out their contracts. It's not a bad life at all, with their kind of salaries. The living is really high off the hog. It must be some kind of justice, after all those glorious days of empire when England sent her younger sons and unwanted officers to the colonies, that now a former colony is returning the favor by sending their unwanted elders.

While it's a good deal for the deportee, it's not such a great deal for the foreign office that falls heir to them. In most cases, they are ill-suited for the jobs they are dropped into, and have little or no interest in them. And even in the case of one man I know who is doing a really good job, the English resent them and count the days till the end of their contracts. It's unfair to the London office when these grizzled retainers don't do a good job, and it's sadly unfair to the man when he does a good job and even the people he brings in and promotes have little or no loyalty to him. In the long run, it would be better for all concerned if these men were allowed to work out their contracts in the peace and quiet of the Racquet Club locker room. After all, you remember what happened to the colonies as a result of this same staffing procedure.

Ironically, most of these men served tours of duty in England during World War II. At that time, the British complaint about them was that they were overpaid, oversexed, and over there. Now their complaint is that they're overpaid, overage and over there. We seem to manage to keep our reputation as big spenders if nothing else.

But it's not these men who are cutting the wide swath in London, it's girls like Anne. A pretty blonde little thing, she'd been knocking out slice of life commercials for P&G at a New York agency with a salary of close to twenty thousand a year. She vacationed once in England and met Prince Charming. He talks and looks like something Central Casting might have sent over for a drawing room comedy. You keep expecting him to say, "Tennis, anyone?" Instead of a court match, he suggests something more intimate: marriage. It's the kind of offer any girl who had been fed a steady diet of Manhattan homosexuals, married men, and mamma's boys would find irresistible. And so she stores her Louis XIV treasures in a warehouse, gives up her rent-controlled pad in the East 50's, and takes off for the UK.

Because young love is such a demanding thing, she did not wait to arrange a transfer from the home office, but flew off into his arms and a job at an American-affiliated agency at an English salary. Only true love could have gotten her through that first winter in London. At a salary of less than half what she'd been making in New York, she could hardly spring for much in the way of living conditions.

She made do with a flat in Chelsea, heavy on atmosphere and charm, but light on more basic things such as heat and privacy. All the rooms opened off a center hall which would have been a marvelously convenient arrangement but for the fact the stairway to the flat above also went through that same hallway. In the middle of the night, a fridge raid might throw you into fairly intimate contact with all kinds of total strangers as well as neighbors between your bedroom and your kitchen. At first she made some sort of attempt to lock each door as she

225

closed it behind her, but the weight of all those keys hanging chatelaine fashion from her belt proved too tiring. She gave that up and threw herself into a kind of open house life style. (And this for a girl who had round the clock doormen, a huge dog, and three locks on her apartment in New York.) But for a while it was all made bearable by the fact that she and he would soon be sharing the family castle and such minor inconveniences would soon be forgotten.

They may be more reticent, harder to get to know, and better looking in tweeds, but Englishmen share certain characteristics with men everywhere. So one particularly damp and clammy day, he told her he was marrying someone else the next weekend.

"Someone I've known for years, actually," he told her.

Someone he'd impregnated the month before, actually, he didn't tell her. So there she was with an ocean between herself, her friends, her French Provincial furniture, and a living wage. But these migratory birds are made of hearty stock, and it wasn't to be an unhappy ending after all. She changed jobs for an enormous increase in salary, purchased a really dreamy flat for herself, complete with all the conveniences the British find so unnecessary, and she's found a chap a bit shorter on lineage but a lot longer on character. And now London's her town.

CHAPTER XXIII

You Don't Have To Be Black To Enjoy Prejudice

Representative Shirley Chisholm, who happens to be in the position of being both black and female, claims that prejudice against women is by far the worse of the two—perhaps because it has had such a marvelous period of uninterrupted growth and maturity. At any rate, it has been around long enough and has been widely accepted enough to have developed sly and subtle niceties that younger and more robust biases can't hope to equal.

Then, too, there is this widely-held belief—oddly enough held by some women as well—that there is something natural or God-given about the inequality of the sexes. There seems to be this almost holy crusade on the part of some men who feel that women were created an inferior breed and it is their duty to keep them in this state of second-class citizenship. So a man who would never in a million years admit a prejudice against blacks or Jews or Catholics, quite openly expresses his prejudices against women in his conversation and in his working arrangements. Men who wouldn't dare laugh at the black liberation movement find something oddly laughable about the women's liberation movement. Or is that perhaps a nervous giggle? The fairer sex didn't get that appellation because of their looks—they got it by comparison with the only other sex around, a sex that makes unfairness to women a way of life.

In the make-believe world of advertising where everything is an exaggeration of real life, you can imagine the delicate refinements that have been added to the basic prejudice ploy. You'll find prejudice against women in such small but basic things as plumbing (the conference rooms of a Park Avenue agency have urinals discreetly tucked into adjoining closets) and such big and baroque items as chair*men* of the board. But it makes itself most powerfully felt in the area of compensation. And not just on the straight salary basis, either.

When I was at D'Arcy they had one of the most elaborately rigged pension plans for the submission of the second sex since the Swiss constitution. Women had to be thirty-five years of age to begin participating in it, men had only to be twenty-one; women had to work there for five consecutive years before becoming eligible to participate; men began participating in it from the first day. Now I don't want you to think for one minute that during those first five years when a woman wasn't participating in all those goodies, she was allowed to sit around munching bonbons and reading French novels. She was expected to work every bit as hard as any man was; she just wasn't expected to be paid as well.

The Fair Employment Practices law made great reading on the front pages of all the liberal newspapers when it was passed, but beyond that it had little or no effect on the openly practiced prejudice against women in advertising (and I would suspect in any other field). Anyone who thinks he can legislate fair play in employment practices is as far off the mark as those stalwarts of an earlier age who thought they could legislate liquor out of the corner bar.

The really amazing thing about prejudice against women is that you find it not just among men, but among members of the so-called weaker sex. This is probably some form of reverse women's lib, or else a deeply confused belief in the movement: If prejudice against women is being practiced by men, they figure, it should be practiced by women too; it's only fair. Whatever the reasoning behind it, it's as easy to come by on Madison Avenue as a disgruntled client.

I remember one wonderfully pleasant interview with a female executive of McCann-Erickson. We had great rapport right from the start; she liked what she saw in my proof book and I had just the right kind of account background to fit the slot that was open in her group. I'd even written on an insurance account—a real rarity for a woman. She'd have hired me in a minute she told me, but unfortunately I was a woman and she didn't want another woman in her group.

A friend of mine, who had the perfect background and qualifications to fit a media opening at Wells, Rich, Greene, was told by the lady herself that the only reason she wasn't being hired was because she was a woman and she didn't want the place to get known as a lady's agency. Can you imagine a guy being turned down for a job because the chairman of the board is afraid the agency will get to be known as a man's agency? When questioned by *Advertising Age* on the subject of prejudice against women, Miss Wells was quoted as saying, "Absolute rot. I've never been discriminated against in my life, and I think the women who have experienced it would have anyway—no matter if they were men or cows or what have you." I guess recognizing discrimination depends a lot on which end of the stick you're on. As 1970's Advertising Woman of the Year, Amelia Bassin said in a speech to the *Advertising Age* Creative Workshop, "It's difficult to tell if success has spoiled Mary Wells, but boy, is she ever spoiling success!"

Betty Corwin, a management consultant and no mean achiever as an executive herself, has said, "A woman has to be twice as good as a man to hold the same job." It's all part of the same syndrome that makes agencies feel a woman should be paid less for equal work.

The things that are sometimes expected of a woman in a position of any clout at an agency are sometimes mind-boggling. I remember a few years back, a feverish worship of motherhood swept through the conference rooms along the Avenue. Any woman who wanted to have her say, or wanted to have her way with a headline or a campaign, had to be a bona fide mother. A woman who wasn't a mother couldn't speak for or to the mothers of America was the reasoning of men who, although they'd never tried motherhood themselves, were convinced *they* could rap with Mrs. Consumer—no problem at all.

Any woman who hadn't already had a child felt obliged to rush into motherhood just to hold her own at copy meetings. Little 3 by 5 inch snapshots of the tots were replaced by 12 by 14 inch studio shots of the small ones all over offices along the Avenue. A friend of mine came out of a meeting just before we lunched one day and said, "I'm not going to any more meetings and listen to any more of that motherhood drivel until I have a baby of my own." Whether or not she went to any meetings in the next nine months or not, I can't vouch for. But it speaks well of her determination that nine months later she produced a son, now my godchild, and we both feel free to attend meetings. I doubt if there are any accurate statistics on the subject, but the birth rate along the Avenue must have taken a sharp turn upward during that year. Not everyone opted for the nine-month wait. That same year Mary Wells adopted her two children. Now with all the pressure on about the population explosion, of course, there is a lot less enthusiasm for motherhood along the Avenue. And there are all those ladies, going home to little ones that were such status symbols in the early sixties.

230

Despite all that is done to denigrate them and keep them in as lowly a state as is allowable under the law, certain women do make it to the top and even more make it to near the top along Madison Avenue. There was a whole generation of flower-hatted lady VPs who got their start when all the men went off to fight World War II. With no one there to keep them in their place, the work and talent of these women brought them the rewards of money and titles they so richly deserved. But in the late fifties and the early sixties, there was a concerted purge of these ladies, and with very few exceptions they are no more. Retirement—like greatness—is often forced upon you.

I was at Benton & Bowles at the time, and we had three lady vice presidents in our creative department. A new head of all creation was brought in from the Midwest, and I guess out there in Pioneerland the ladies stuck pretty much to their stitching and kitchens. The sight of that many women running around in something other than calico was more than he could take. And within a very few weeks, all three of these ladies were not only without their titles, but without their jobs as well.

At another big P&G agency up the road a piece, the squeeze on the ladies has been a slower one, but it has been just as effective. The big soap companies, by the sheer weight of their advertising budgets and their acceptance of lady creative types, have probably done more for freeing women than the inventor of the washing machine. If a woman writes on a soap account long enough (and that's usually at least twice as long as it takes a man to accomplish the same thing), she eventually so endears herself to the soap men that they expect her to receive some kind of recognition from her agency. The organizational ladder is as rigid in the big companies as it is in the army: Assistant brand men talk to assistant account executives, brand men talk to account executives, and vice presidents—like the Cabots and the Lodges—talk only to each other. To match the vice presidents on the company side of the table, the agency has to mount an equally impressive array of titles on its side of the table. And that's how a few of the ladies with the VPs made it. They've got the titles, and they get to talk to other vice presidents, but in most cases that's about as far as it goes. The clout that usually goes with that title just doesn't seem to attach itself when the titleholder's a lady. Neither the clout nor the salary. But women have for so many uncounted generations been brought up to expect so little that we take great pride even in this tokenism.

Just how powerless these ladies are was made clear by a management consultant who told me that whenever an agency with an entrenched creative head wanted to spruce up its creative image without rocking the boat, they looked for a woman to fill the number two spot in the creative department. That way they could parade a really creative image around without any serious threat to the entrenched top creative guy. "When they want a number one talent in a number two spot, they choose a woman, knowing she's no threat."

At a recent luncheon given by the Advertising Women of New York, the topic discussed was "The Liberation Movement As It Affects Ad Media." One of the exhibits was a reel of current commercials. After they were shown, there was a general hue and cry from the assembled lovelies about the rampant sexism in many of them. The ladies in particular objected to the showing of women—in soap commercials and in others—as less than bright in some cases and downright idiotic in others.

To me, they seemed to be missing the point, and on shaky ground as well. For in Videoland, men fare no better than women in being cast as fools. Sexism in commercials is just as

232

subtle and devious as racism has always been. It's not so much how you show women, it's how you don't show them. With 45 per cent of the female population working, the advertiser still refuses to show women in executive positions. If he is willing to show a female more than an apron string's length from her washer-dryer, he shows her as a secretary—never as an executive, never as a pediatrician, never as a lawyer. No wonder little girls grow up with such foreshortened ambitions. The wonder is that so many of them ever do make it out of the kitchen and the typing pool.

A friend of mine who has worked in advertising both in this country and abroad said she found Europe surprisingly free of any prejudice against *American* women in advertising. They find it harder than we do to accept their own women in executive positions, but they readily accept American women in almost any kind of executive job because they feel American women are a breed apart. It should only be true!

But the prejudice against women doesn't stop at limiting their executive powers. It gets right down to the nitty-gritty of everyday routine matters. Take expense accounts. (If you're smart you'll take a man's, not a woman's.) At one big Madison Avenue shop, there's one set of rules for men's expense accounts and another for women's. A friend of mine who was on a location job, shooting a commercial for this agency, said she didn't care that the account executive was putting in for—and collecting on—big entertainment and dinner tabs every night since he was in charge of keeping the client happy. But when they objected to a 75¢ charge on her account for one night when she took herself to the movies (75¢—that's how deep into the woods they were on this location), that really was the last straw.

With such a diversity of prejudice to enjoy, it's not surprising that women in advertising—and I expect elsewhere—react

233

in equally diverse ways. They become outrageously unfeminine, aping men in their less attractive, more aggressive characteristics. Or they swing in the opposite direction and hide behind a fluffy facade of femininity that appears too goody-two-shoes to be true, and usually is. No matter which of these paths she chooses, she is invariably criticized. But have you ever heard a man criticized because he was too ambitious, too aggressive, or even too sexy?

CHAPTER XXIV

How I Got Resigned

"I was shocked to hear you've resigned," the art director said to me.

"Don't give it a second thought," I assured him. "I'm a little upset, but I haven't resigned."

But by the time the third person had called me that afternoon to say how dismayed he was that I'd resigned, I decided to trace the rumor back to its source. It was Harry, the hatchet man for the new order that claimed they were making a clean sweep of the creative department. (Never put a broom or a hatchet in the hands of the untrained—he was also sweeping out half of the agency's accounts. But no matter.)

"Listen, Harry, stop telling people I resigned," I used as an opener.

"But I've accepted your resignation," the hatchet riposted.

"You can't accept a resignation I never offered! Now you get back on the phone and call all those people and admit that you fired me."

It wasn't a conversation that you were likely to hear often on Madison Avenue, but it gave me a perverse kind of thrill. In an industry where resignations are almost invariably the front for a lot of unpleasantness, I wanted no part of it. The hatchet and I were toe to toe on the issue because I wanted to assure myself a warm welcome from the friendly folks at the Unemployment Office, and he wanted a nice safe excuse to give to all my accounts who would undoubtedly be asking after me.

It took me two hysterical meetings and a lot of memos, but I finally got fired. Except for the resignation aspect of it, it hadn't come completely as a surprise. I had been warned by one of my account supervisors, a vice president who was out on the West Coast shooting some commercials I had written for SCM. (Don't ask why he, not me—that's another story.) He'd called in one day to say that the creative director was after my neck because the client had chosen my commercials over his (in an unmarked blindfold test called a work session).

"Watch yourself crossing streets," he told me. "He's really out to get you." The VP, a Latin type, always had had a flair for the dramatic and I dismissed his warning. Actually he had understated the case. Not only had SCM bought my commercials over the creative director's, but the following week Knox did the same thing. His reasoning seemed to be that if I was gone they'd have to buy his commercials. He figured wrong, though, because shortly after I left, the accounts were gone, too. In all fairness, I've got to admit that the mass exodus of clients was probably more due to his staying than my leaving, since accounts I'd never laid a pen to left, too.

People who have lived through both tell me getting fired is in one respect like an automobile accident: They're both terrible ways to stop. Those same people have no desire to repeat either of the experiences and, if forced to choose between reliving one or the other, claim they'd be hard-pressed to make a choice.

There once was a gaggle of Hollywood writers who were known for their ability to construct "the cute meet." They

236

were much in demand when Doris Day movies were big on the circuits. Now advertising has the reputation of being the business for "the cute firing." Stories abound, hopefully many of them apocryphal, about the funny, bitter, ironic, or just plain crazy ways people have been fired—from the one about the girl who got it under the dryer at Bendel's, to the one who finally forced her supervisor into firing her because she overused the phrase, "My analyst says my writing blocks are all your fault," to the BBDO writer who was fired by telegram on location. He'd heard weeks earlier that he was going to be dropped, decided to make himself scarce around the office, and began following around one location crew after another.

Don't misunderstand me. I'm not recommending getting fired as a way of life; I'm just saying it isn't all bad. It was my first such experience, and it opened up a whole new way of life called "the interview."

Although I was writing, editing, and directing a film for the USIA at the time, I felt a strange compulsion to go out on an endless series of interviews. Some Puritan ethic kept forcing me to seek a nine to five job, although I was at the time working anywhere from five to sixteen hours a day on the film. In fact it was not until after the film was finished and I had taken to my bed with my SCM, determined to become the Harold Robbins of Sutton Place, that I finally was able to break myself of the interview habit, limiting them at that time to 4 p.m. and later. Notwithstanding the Puritan drive that had me convinced nice girls don't earn a living in bed (even if they are alone with a typewriter), I really was enjoying the interviews. While everyone who interviewed me could scarcely have passed as the salt of the earth, there were still quite a few nice ones in the crowd. I met some marvelous people and some perfect turds, too, but taken as a whole, there were enough charmers in the crowd to make the experience a positive one.

237

Not all my friends share my high regard for the interview as a pastime. Maybe they've just run into more clinkers than I have. One certainly did. From the opening remarks, she knew this interview was not going to mark any high point for those keeping track of such things. She realized her initial intuitive reaction had been right when the prospective employer fixed her with a beady eye and announced, "I wouldn't want my wife to work." She kept a cool head and even resisted the impulse to snap back, "And I wouldn't want my husband to be rude to any woman he was considering employing." Now the mother of two, this same friend of mine told me that before she'd had children, at least once in every interview she'd be asked, "Are you planning on having any children?" or the even ruder, "Why haven't you and your husband had any children?" If those same interviewers tried that question on a male applicant, they'd have ended up with a fat lip. Actually, the hardest part of some interviews is staying polite.

The hardest part of one interview I went through was staying awake. The interviewer had evidently prepared a set speech—that's right, speech not questions—and he planned to get through it within a fixed time. He placed his watch on his desk and began. After a few minutes of this, I was beginning to feel a little left out and kind of sorry I hadn't brought my typewriter—or at least a notebook—with me. To indicate that I was still there and still interested, I tried to ask a couple of questions, but these were brushed aside and I was told he'd get to that later. It was only then that I realized that somewhere inside this man was a recorded announcement, and there was going to be no give and take until it had run its course. When the invisible interior tape finally did run out, he turned out to be a perfectly nice guy.

While married ladies looking for employment have to put up with being grilled about their fertility or lack of it, single women have other harrowing questions to face. I remember being cross-examined during one interview:

"Are you now married?"

"No."

"Have you ever been married?"

"No."

"Well, why isn't a nice girl like you married?" (You know, if the guy who originated that line was getting residuals, he'd be the richest man in the world.)

All the smart-ass answers that you've always used in reply to this chestnut cross your mind, but basically he's a nice guy so you cool them. Later in the interview the question came up again, but only after he'd asked me my favorite restaurants and what plays I'd seen lately. I was sure he wouldn't offer me the job but would probably ask me out to dinner—I was wrong on both counts.

Some of the people who interviewed me I'd have liked under any circumstances. That I can vouch for because the interview as a social custom leaves a lot to be desired. One man who interviewed me three times became a special favorite. During the course of our interviews he rose from somewhere in the creative department at Y&R to president of another agency, and I wrote three novels. He never liked my proof book well enough to buy it, but he has promised to buy all my novels. It's only fair.

Even fairer was a man for whom I will always have a warm spot in my heart. I was about halfway through a seemingly endless series of interviews at one company, when he took me to breakfast to psyche me for the next interview. I'll always be grateful to him.

I'm not the only one who thinks interviews can be fun, because "Just looking, thanks" interviews are epidemic in the business. Writers often take part in them just to bolster their egos. If you've got a good book, it's nice to hear someone say flattering things about you and your work; a good interview can set you up for days. And there's always the chance the job they offer will be one you'll want.

The lookers, though, are not only the writers. Lots of times the interviewer is "Just looking, thanks". And he can be doing it for several reasons: He may be hard-pressed for some fresh ideas and hopes he'll be able to find them in an outsider's book. Or he may be looking at your book as a favor to a mutual friend.

The minute the word gets out that you are on the beach or seriously looking, every friend insists on setting up interviews for you. Ninety-nine per cent of these obligatory interviews are at agencies where there are no openings at the time. Not only do these interviews waste the writer's time, but they can work against you in the long run. When a spot does open up at that agency, no flesh peddler will send you over to it if he knows you've already seen anyone at that agency.

When you're new at the interview game, you're not always quite sure of what you're getting into. You look around an agency when you step off the elevator and try to make an educated guess about the kind of writer they're after. If you step into a reception room filled with lots of chromium, glass, and sharp colors, you can expect your creative types to be dressed like beachcombers or gypsies. Once I found myself being interviewed at an agency, with the full Knoll Associate look in the lobby, by a creative director in garishly striped bell bottoms and a carefully faded denim shirt open to his waist. He looked like he'd just stepped off the Fire Island ferry—right down to his bare feet.

Sheraton or Chippendale knock-offs usually indicated a more conservative bent and more interest in the successful campaigns you've written than in your ability to pass as someone from Central Casting. But you can't always judge an agency by its decor. One of the most sophisticated of all palace revolutions took place in the homespun early American atmosphere of Y&R. Funny thing happened to a friend of mine there. She showed up for an interview with Al Hampel, not realizing that the creative floor looked more like something out of Sturbridge Village than Madison Avenue. Sorry that she hadn't thought to wear calico, she beat her way through the chintz and curly maple to his office, threw herself down in a Windsor reproduction, and tried for a light note. Glancing around at the excesses of early Americana, she said, "If I'd known, I'd have cross-stitched my résumé." She didn't get a smile or the job, but considered it a small loss.

A young friend of mine who looks a bit like she might have just stepped off the pages of *Seventeen* or *Mademoiselle* has been specializing, logically enough, in fashion copy since graduating from the Fashion Institute of Technology. She is always the first with the latest; hers were the miniest, the midiest, and naturally she was the first kid in her copy group to get into hot pants. Anyhow, when you look like that, you learn to expect a lot of reaction in interviews. She said she thought she was prepared for just about everything (having already fielded questions about how she would handle a proposition from a client at the interview for her last job). But her most recent interview topped them all. She was called back three times to one agency on a copy-contact job. The creative guy loved her stuff, but the account manager evidently had his doubts. Each time he saw her, he looked at her with a more puzzled look.

"Is there something bothering you about me?" she finally asked him.

"Well, I've got no doubts about you being able to handle the job, but I'll tell you frankly (that's when she should have left), I've got a client up in Maine who'd have an orgasm if he just laid his eyes on you!" It's not that you're looking for equality in interviews, most of us would settle for civility.

One reason why advertising has been able to develop and perfect the cute or unique firing is that there's so much of it going on, they've really gotten good at it. The number of people on the beach along the Avenue makes Coney Island on a Saturday in July look deserted. When a big account pulls out, a lot of people lose their jobs. It can be as simple as that. Or when a new head of all creation is brought in, there's inevitably a bloodbath. And now that agencies have gone public, with stockholders breathing down their necks for increased profits, the war of attrition has become even bloodier. Nothing boosts stock value like an upturn in profits. And if a quarter has not seen the addition of enough new business to give the profits a healthy boost, there's only one way to produce the increased earnings. You cut costs. When an agency announces an increase in profits of 90 per cent in one period as Wells, Rich, Greene did in September '70, you know they didn't make savings like that just conserving on erasers and pencils. They cut the payroll and they cut it big. It was a technique that became an epidemic along the Avenue that year—major surgery on the personnel list and salary cutbacks for a lot of those who stayed. (An interesting footnote to the 1970 sinking spell was the fact that of the ten biggest agencies, only Ted Bates did not cut personnel, but actually added over 250 to its staff.) With so much pressure on the agencies to engage in firing, it's no small wonder that they have honed the techniques as marvelously as they have.

At Benton & Bowles, where they've had even more practice than most agencies in the past couple of years, they've developed a gang war system of elimination that is both neat and effective. Writers and art directors not assigned to a specific account are called in, put on teams, and given the assignment of coming up with something new. You gotta pray you're not on the team of the guy they're after. According to the rules of the game, no matter what his team produces, it's invariably received with the line, "Is that all you can come up with?" Don't ask for whom the knell tolls—it tolls for the whole team.

One of the seamier sides of being fired is being thrown into the hands of the personnel agents. If the people who interview you range from disastrous to delightful, the people who set up the interviews run a shorter gamut from irritating to insidious. These headhunters came into unprecedented prominence during the youthquake, when each had a stable of brash young writers willing to play musical chairs. One lady of the profession became notorious for this technique: By moving these kids from agency to agency before their lack of results showed up, and by demanding larger and larger salaries for them on each move, she developed her string of over-priced talent. And the game went on until well into 1970 when the agencies, pressed to the wall, were looking for results not footwork.

So powerful did some of these placement people become during the sixties that writers, an insecure lot at best, often felt a greater loyalty to the headhunter who had placed them than to the agency where they were working. This wasn't a reciprocal loyalty, unfortunately, and it made for some pretty sticky situations. One of these headhunters once called a writer at BBDO and said she was setting up an appointment for her at Ogilvy. The appointment was set for the noon hour (after all, she was still working at BBDO) and the same day as the appointment, the headhunter called the writer's boss at BBDO to say that she had heard the writer in question was unhappy and looking around, and that she—the one who had set the appointment for the writer—had three applicants, any one of

243

whom would be perfect for the writer's job at BBDO. Fortunately the girl got the job at Ogilvy, because she came back that afternoon to a nasty atmosphere at BBDO. Flesh peddling from the days of the triangle trade in rum, sugarcane, and slaves has never been a pretty profession.

CHAPTER XXV

Some of My Best Friends Still Are

. . . in advertising. And if they haven't made it into this book, it's only because they make better friends than copy.

If there have been a few sticky moments in all those years in the business, on balance they were still great, and I'm as convinced as ever, it sure beats working for a living. Now having worked both sides of the Avenue, the agency's and the client's, I've got to admit it's just as much fun on the client's side and the breathing's a lot easier.

But there were days at the agencies I wouldn't have wanted to be any place else on earth; days when an ad you've written moves a product into first place, or doubles the sales of a long established company, or when the president of the insurance account you work on orders a thousand reprints of a trade ad you did for distribution among his pals at the yacht club. If you don't get a kick out of things like that, you don't belong in the business.

And though it's become de rigueur to roll your eyes toward the ceiling and moan about the pressures of the business, there are always enough beautiful lulls between the panics (assuming you've picked your agency with any care at all) to make the livin' if not easy, at least enjoyable.

Though some of my best friends are still on the Avenue, many are not. Account losses, office politics, and in some cases skyrocketing blood pressure have forced some of them into other fields. The areas they chose to move into are as varied as the ways in which people get into advertising. There's an account man running a successful ski lodge in New England; an associate creative director at BBDO happily running a chichi restaurant in the Hamptons; an art director who found a ready market for her handcrafted leather things at Bendel's; a creative director who started buying condominiums and ended up the mini-Zeckendorf of the East Side; a copy supervisor and bird watcher who is now happy as a clam at high tide writing endless novels and editing bird books. Sometimes what starts as a hobby or moonlighting while you're still on the Avenue becomes so intriguing or so demanding that you're forced to turn to it full time. That's what happened to the B&B writer whose big prize-winning novel started out being written evenings, then two days a week, until finally he gave up his job to devote his full time to it.

Among the people who have left Madison Avenue, the difference between the bitter and the better-off seems to be more in mental attitude than in monetary matters. To come out of it unscathed, you've got to have a fallback position, a secretly developed talent or business or a really rich daddy. The biggest mistake too many people make about the garden of delights along Madison Avenue is that it's a permanent thing.

It isn't permanent, but it *is* a garden of real delights. Along its path have bloomed hearty perennials from Bernice Fitzgibbons and Jean Rindlaub through Jane Trahey to Mary Wells and Shirley Polykoff. And though they've sunk deep and seemingly permanent roots into the Avenue, I really think the key to enjoying the neighborhood pleasures is to keep in mind their transiency.

Once you realize Madison Avenue is a good address but a temporary one, you're home free. Provided you can pay the rent.